KURVES!
THE MUSICAL

Book, Music & Lyrics by

Amy Shojai & Frank Steele

CONTACT:

SHOJAI & STEELE PLAYS
P.O. BOX 1904
SHERMAN TX 75091-1904

Amy Shojai
amy@shojai.com
903-868-1022

Frank Steele
the.steeles@verizon.net
903-893-2039

DIRECTOR'S NOTES

KURVES is a two-hour musical comedy in two acts, featuring 12 songs and eight actors onstage virtually the whole time. The play is set in Kurves, Texas and takes place early one morning when a group of misfits get locked inside a woman's gym. Despite failed attempts to find happiness they finally succeed—but in unexpected ways.

In **ACT ONE**, we learn that wise-cracking Maxine (played by a man) has owned the gym for 30 years. Three regulars arrive. Mabel is the many-times-married director of a soup kitchen who despite her drill-sergeant demeanor is a softie who collects human strays needing help. Old maid poetry teacher Jane wants to make an impression at her next high school reunion because she's always felt invisible (song: **SOMEONE MUST SEE ME**). Newlywed Ronnie from the wrong side of the tracks married the "town catch" Troy but lied about being pregnant and feels unworthy of his love (song: **THE PICTURE**).

Two inept small-time thieves, Boots and Fingers, attempt to rob the women. Boots fancies himself a dancer and ladies' man and wants a fancy car to attract the woman of his dreams. Fingers carries his treasures in his Superman lunchbox and has always been the butt of jokes but just wants a purpose in life (song/duet: **PITCHING WOO**). The pair cut the phone line, tape up the women and deposit swiped jewelry into Finger's lunchbox while Boots hits on the women with groaner pick-up lines (song/dance: **YOU'RE THE CHICK FOR ME**).

Quizzed about a mysterious past, Maxine reveals a long-ago love disappeared when life threw unexpected curves (song: **CURVES**). After glitzy bitchy visitor Celia arrives at the gym for a workout, Boots locks the door to prevent future interruptions and breaks the key, trapping everyone inside. Fingers and Boots exit to try and get out the jammed back door.

Celia is recognized as a famous TV motivational speaker. She gives Jane and Ronnie a pep talk (song/trio: **DREAMS FOR SALE**), but Celia admits to herself that she's tired of being a fake, but doesn't know how to stop. Meanwhile Maxine recognizes Celia as his lost love but fears revealing the truth.

When Boots and Fingers return to the stage the women tie them up. Celia reclaims her "sparkles" and Fingers recognizes her ring-necklace matches Maxine's—and the jig is up when Celia recognizes Max as her long-lost fiancé. In the finale, each character complains the others "have it better" (song/company: **LIFE HAPPENS**). Maxine becomes Max when he removes his wig, shocking everyone that he's a man, just as the lights go down.

ACT TWO opens with Celia anguished by Max's betrayal. She laments her lost 30 years and demands an explanation (song/duet: **THE DREAM**). Mabel gets fed up with everyone's pity party complaints, and all but Celia "confess" and receive gospel-style pep talks from Mabel (song/Company: **SUCK IT UP, SWEETHEART**).

Max explains his disappearance and begs for another chance with Celia. But after 30 years of silence, she can't trust his story that he disappeared to protect her. The previous gym owner wouldn't sell to a man so he masqueraded as a woman to hide from the mob because "that's how witness protection works."

Mabel wants to help lovable simple Fingers but without insulting him (song/duet: **PITCHING WOO**, reprise) when he explains movies help him find the right words (song: **SILVER SCREEN BLUES**). Fingers agrees to take a job at the soup kitchen to help kids find and recognize their own treasures.

Jane and Boots are smitten, delighted to find each other and that finally someone "sees" and appreciates them. Jane agrees to help Boots become more refined if he'll teach her how to put jazz in her life (song/duet: **POETRY & JAZZ**).

Ronnie the romantic scolds Celia for not accepting a "real life fairytale come true" when they've actually got a second chance at love. Celia wants to give Max (and herself) one more chance (song: **AM I HAPPY?**) but fears being hurt again.

Ronnie's husband TROY bursts through the back door, looking for his wife—he knows the trick for opening the lock. Ronnie fearfully admits she's not pregnant, but he doesn't care, and professes his love (song/duet: **THE PICTURE**, reprise). He's the assistant DA and tells about just recovered mob money that's been traced to the mafia hit man Max testified against 30 years ago. They learn that Max could have come out of hiding 15 years earlier. Celia realizes Max's outrageous story is true.

Fingers asks if Celia and Max will reconcile after all these years (song/company: **CURVES** reprise). Everyone prepares to go home—in couples—and Celia admits she's already home. She gives Jane her sparkly coat as she's "out grown it" so Jane truly becomes the girl with the sparkles. The entire company discovers they finally grabbed and caught the brass ring (song/company: **LIFE HAPPENS**, reprise).

CHARACTER BREAKDOWNS

MAXINE (MAX) SPINALTI (BARITONE) is a working class guy. He worked in the family shop to save money and give his fiancée Celia the life she deserves. But after seeing a murder, he's thrust into witness protection and never gets to say goodbye or explain when he's relocated. He buys a down-and-out women's exercise club, MAXINE'S to establish a new life—the original owner would only sell to a woman so he played that role—and now can't change. He still wears Celia's ring on a chain around neck (ring is VITAL to character). There is a lot of hidden depth to Max, but he likes to keep things on a superficial level. Max's wise-ass attitude hides a lot of pain and insecurity in his life. It takes a while for us to see the real Max. This character should NOT be played as a drag queen. Max and Celia end up together; cast age-appropriate actors—the amount of time they've been separated can be adjusted, based on the age of the actors cast.

MABEL DeLOUISE BELEW FELCHER CALVIN (ALTO, WITH BELT) has been married and lost husbands four times (that people know of) and is now one of the richest people in town. She has a drill sergeant demeanor that keeps most people at a distance, and she's something of a mystery to even those who have known her for years. She's always wanted to be a mom, but by the time she found and married the love of her life Rev. Calvin, it was too late. Mabel runs the local soup kitchen, won't tolerate cussing, collects human "strays" and constantly "fixes" others' problems because she's good at it and it's easier than getting them to fix themselves. Fingers' innocent "please like me" attitude brings out her "inner mom" and she sees in him the child she always wanted. Fingers inspires her to encourage others to suck it up and fix themselves instead of relying on her—or others—for their happiness. Mabel is imposing and must appear to be the oldest character and she should be able to sing convincing gospel/bluesy licks.

VERONICA "RONNIE" NOONAN (2ND SOPRANO) is a sweet but poor have-not from the wrong side of the tracks, but much smarter and prettier than she realizes. She recently married "above her station" to the town's golden boy, who is the assistant DA. She thinks he went with her just to spite his parents and married her because she got pregnant—a lie instigated by Ronnie's manipulative mom. Ronnie desperately wants to get pregnant to ensure their love and so he won't discover her lie and leave. She's eaten up with guilt, but also love-struck and insecure, and is losing weight to please her mother-in-law. She just wants to be loved—at any cost—and must learn to trust that her Cinderella dream is the real thing. She starts out as shy, insecure with low self-esteem and transforms into a strong, determined and confident young woman able to inspire change in others. Ronnie is the youngest character, probably a couple years out of high school and about 5-10 years younger than her husband.

JANE DOUGH (SOPRANO) literally is a "plain Jane." She's mousy, wears no makeup, her hair is a Frankenstein experiment gone bad because she doesn't think anything can help so no longer tries—she's always felt invisible to others. She's a high school teacher passionate about poetry, oblivious to the fact that kids adore her (including former student Ronnie), and she's the ONE teacher everyone will remember because she cares so much and makes a difference in lives. Jane's determined to re-make herself and finally be noticed at her 25th high school reunion where she was just one of the crowd. She's tickled that Boots finds her attractive—and actually becomes beautiful when his attentions make her feel pretty. It's not makeup or hairstyle, but the possibility of happiness and newfound confidence that ultimately transforms her into a beauty. Actress should have major singing chops, operatic aria style but able to "jazz" it up. She should seem old enough to have been Ronnie's high school teacher—you may adjust the reunion year to match age of the actress.

DANNY (BOOTS) BLOOTMAN (BARI-TENOR) loves to dance (not necessarily well) and dresses fairly well for a low-level crook (aka "Saturday Night Fever). He's not overly bright, but fancies himself a ladies' man. He tries to be smooth, but it just doesn't read. Danny doesn't know or recognize rejection. He sees every lady in Maxine's as fair game, but uses the oldest lines in the world to woo them. The mere presence of any woman makes Danny lose focus on his mission. He wants to buy a sexy car so the ladies will like him, but Danny isn't a typical sex-obsessed guy. He truly wants a good woman, but his methods are comical, yet sad. The humor comes from his earnest approach. He's never to be glaringly "out there" and there's almost a Barney Fife genuineness to his approach. He's not a bad person, just a desperate person, and there's a sweetness revealed once Jane reciprocates interest. Ability to move/dance a plus but not required—acting ability is more important. Be aware that Danny and Jane end up together and cast actors accordingly.

WILLY (FINGERS) MULROY (BARI-TENOR) is pure comic relief—at least that's what we think at first. He's funny, incompetent, goofy, and tries to be tough. But real guns frighten him so he uses his hidden finger in a pocket during stick-ups. Willy goes along with more forceful characters because he wants to be liked. He has never been much of a success at anything—he's not so much a loser as just a bad luck kind of guy. Anything he's ever done has been for the good of others, and that includes robbery. We like Willy, and he should never be played as a stereotypical "dumb guy." His child-like sweetness is endearing, and no one ever must fear Willy. He knows he's not great in the brains department but loves old films, feels awed by actors who always know what to say at the right time. Fingers uses movie lines and film titles in conversation to boost his IQ quotient (sometimes they work, most times not). He wants to be a good person and have a purpose but doesn't know how—and Mabel gives him the means to help others and make a difference. Cast any age or any "type"—think of interesting combinations with Boots and/or with Mabel. Note that Fingers sings a killer blues solo and gospel with Mabel.

CELIA LOVEJOY, (1ST SOPRANO) a stranger passing through town, dresses "uptown" with lots of flashy jewelry, and appears bitchy, brittle, and gives nothing away. She sells dreams as a motivational speaker, and hosts a popular self-help TV program. Celia stops at Maxine's before traveling to her next speaking engagement. She wants to believe in the possibility of happiness and can put on an act—but no longer believes her own spiel. She's traded success for happiness after she lost her soul-mate 30 years ago. Celia still wears a simple ring on a chain he gave her (ring is VITAL to character). When she recognizes Max as her lost love she's devastated, incensed, and ultimately saved—and gives up EVERYTHING for a last chance of happiness when she learns love can survive despite time, distance, and silence. Be aware that Max and Celia end up together and cast age-appropriate actors accordingly—the amount of time they've been separated—30 years—can be adjusted up or down based on the age of the actors cast.

TROY CHADWICK NOONAN IV (BARITONE) is the only child of the richest family in town—his father, uncles and cousins are all are either lawyers or judges. Troy was quarterback of football team, president of debate club/student council, and star of high school play. He has the sort of success and life that makes you want to hate him except he's a thoroughly nice guy. He believes strongly in public service and is the youngest assistant DA in the history of the town. Troy's mother believes Ronnie is a gold-digger, and takes every opportunity to put her down, saying his job exposes him to all the wrong kinds of people. But Troy adores Ronnie, says she keeps him grounded in what's important. The actor should be 5 to 10 years older than Ronnie. He does NOT need to be an Adonis, but could be—Ronnie just thinks of him that way because she's in love.

COSTUMES

Maxine: Sweats (well-worn), tennis shoes, wig, padded bra
Mabel: Sweats, tennis shoes
Ronnie: High fashion workout clothes so new you almost see price tag, high dollar shoes
Jane: Sweats (subdued), tennis shoes
Celia: Sweats (flashy), flashy tennis shoes, a lot of conspicuous jewelry.
Boots: White belt and shoes. Leisure suit, or loud sports coat and slacks. That double knit theme, a used car salesman look.
Fingers: Superhero tee-shirt, jeans, tennis shoes. Almost childlike look.
Troy: Nice suit, tie, white shirt "lawyer" look

PERSONAL PROP LIST

Maxine: Ring on string, cash for change, keys on ring, 8 track tapes
Celia: Ring on string, lots of jewelry, key card
Jane: Car keys
Mabel: Cash, wedding ring
Ronnie: Wedding rings
Fingers: Superhero lunch box, photos, movie ticket stubs, watchband/string dog collar

SET PIECES/PROP LIST (general)

Phone (old)
Cash box or Cash Register
"MAXINE'S" sign (optional)
Exercise bike or similar
Stairmaster or similar
Handheld weights/Dumbbells
Area fans (old fashion)
"Body image/eat healthy" wall posters
Desk and Rolling office chair
Clock (can be referred to on "4th wall")
Tape, jump rope, holiday string, etc.
Various 8 tracks
Ledger book

SCENE SYNOPSIS

The action takes place early one morning in Kurves, Texas in a rundown woman's gym.

MUSICAL NUMBERS
Act One

Overture
Auld Lang Syne (workout music)
Someone Must See Me..Jane
The Picture ....Ronnie
Pitching Woo..Fingers, Boots
You're the Chick for Me ....Boots
Curves..Max
Dreams for Sale..Celia, Jane, Ronnie
Life Happens..Company

Act Two

Life Happens (Ent'racte)
The Dream..Max, Celia
Suck It Up, Sweetheart..All but Celia
Pitching Woo (Reprise)...Fingers, Mabel
Silver Screen Blues...Fingers
Poetry & Jazz..Jane, Boots
Happy ....Celia
The Picture (Reprise)...Troy, Ronnie
Curves (Reprise)..Company
Life Happens (Reprise & bows)...Company
Suck It Up, Sweetheart (Reprise/Encore-optional)....................Company

L-R: Leah Martin, Craig Sturm, Amy Shojai, Theresa Littlefield, Joe Maglio, Cheri Anderson, Frank Steele, Johnny Flowers.

PRODUCTION HISTORY:

KURVES, THE MUSICAL was first produced and directed by Amy Shojai and Frank Steele at the Rialto Theater, 424 West Main Street, Denison, Texas on March 1-3, 2012. The cast was as follows (in order of appearance):

```
MAXINE "MAX" ..................................................................Frank Steele
MABEL ..........................................................................Cheri Anderson
RONNIE ...............................................................................Leah Martin
JANE .........................................................................Theresa Littlefield
BOOTS..................................................................................Joe Maglio
FINGERS ........................................................................Johnny Flowers
CELIA..................................................................................Amy Shojai
TROY ..................................................................................Craig Sturm
```

KURVES, THE MUSICAL

L-R: Frank Steele, Joe Maglio, Theresa Littlefield, Amy Shojai, Gil Nelson, Nikki Silva, Hilary Gregory-Allen, Johnny Flowers

The show returned to The Rialto Theater back by popular demand with the original cast plus three *new cast members on October 11-13, 2012. It was again directed by Frank Steele and Amy Shojai. The cast was as follows (in order of appearance):

```
MAXINE "MAX" ...............................................................Frank Steele
MABEL ........................................................................... Nikki Silva*
RONNIE ................................................................ Hilary Gregory-Alan*
JANE ....................................................................Theresa Littlefield
BOOTS...........................................................................Joe Maglio
FINGERS ......................................................................Johnny Flowers
CELIA..........................................................................Amy Shojai
TROY ........................................................................... Gil Nelson*
```

ACT I

Scene 1

The action of the play takes place in Kurves, (YOUR STATE), and the dimly lit stage reveals a rundown women's gym with several exercise machines. It's not dirty, just rundown. A lighted sign identifies the gym as MAXINE'S. There is a desk with an old cash register, a telephone, and scattered papers. Actors appear from back of the theater and enter stage from a doorway (empty door frame) at front of stage. A second doorway upstage leads to another room offstage.

MAXINE (man dressed as woman) enters from back of theater. She is middle age, not too feminine, and as much as she tries, not overly happy. It's 6 a.m. and this is her daily routine. MAXINE unlocks the doorway with large ring of keys. She's on automatic pilot as she turns on lights, switches on MAXINE'S sign, looks in cash drawer, checks 8-track tape selections. Doesn't like any of them, finally settles on one and goes into back room and the exercise music starts—Auld Lang Syne with a beat.

MABEL enters from the rear of theater. She is a formidable woman. She is older, and obviously well to do.

MAXINE
(*Pauses in doorway as music sounds, and speaks just as MABEL enters stage*) How can you work up a sweat to THAT? You just suck!

MABEL
I love you too, sweetheart.

MAXINE
If I was talking to you, Mabel, I would have used stronger language. *(Grins)*

MABEL
My monthly dues are due. Did I just say that? I mean, dues are due now. I mean, I need to pay you for the month, Maxine. Have you got change for a hundred?

MAXINE

I sure do, Mabel. Thought you had me, didn't you? Every month for years, you've pulled this "change for a hundred" stuff. Well, I got you this time. In fact, since it's forty-five bucks a month, would you like to pay for last month and next month, too?

MABEL

(Reluctantly) I guess so.

MAXINE

(Making change) And, here you go. Ten whole dollars back. It kills you, doesn't it? To part with that money?

MABEL

Well….

MAXINE

Oh, c'mon. You've got more money than the Vatican.

MABEL

Don't you dare make fun of the Vatican. Are you calling me rich? *(Almost insulted, and then defensive.)* I'm not rich! I'm. . . I'm comfortable. That's all.

MAXINE

Well, make room in the bed cuz I want to be "comfortable" too.

> *RONNIE enters with JANE. RONNIE is timid, but tries to cover it. She is sweet, but by marrying the town 'catch' she feels out of her element. JANE is plain, painfully so. She has always been invisible.*

RONNIE

Hello, ladies. It's cold out there. Oh, Maxine. Do I owe you money?

MAXINE

No, dear. You know I love you, but you've already lost 25 pounds, what are you doing here? If you do owe money, why not let Mabel pay? She's loaded, you know.

MABEL

Will you just stop that? I told you that I'm--

MAXINE, RONNIE and JANE

(in unison) Comfortable! *(They all laugh)*

JANE

Am I all caught up?

MAXINE
I don't know. I forgot to look at your statement. (*JANE looks dejected*) Here, let me see. . . (*MAXINE doesn't look. She forgets*) Ok, ladies. That equipment isn't gonna exercise by itself. (*MAXINE makes a thumping sound with her hands, and sits at desk to do some busy work. JANE and RONNIE cross to exercise on the other side of stage.*)

JANE
Why does she do that?

RONNIE
What?

JANE
That thing with her hands. Haven't you noticed it before?

RONNIE
No, not really.

JANE
Well, look for it. She does it a lot.

RONNIE
Ok, I will.

MABEL
(*Music stops. Hands on hips*) I didn't like that music anyway. Those old 8-tracks skip more than Richard Simmons on his way to a David Cassidy concert. Maxine, when are you going to get something new?

MAXINE
8-tracks came with the place. You can't find that kind of quality music on CDs.

MABEL
You got that right. (*Pause, to MAXINE*) Does this jogging suit make my butt look big? Please be honest. You can tell me the truth. Don't hold back on me. Does it?

MAXINE
No, Mabel. It doesn't.

MABEL
(*Excited*) Really?

MAXINE
It makes your butt look huge. You look like you've got a sack of grain in your pants.

MABEL
Well, I never in my life!

MAXINE
(*In a teasing wise-ass tone*) Aw, I bet you did! Never what? Never met a cheeseburger you didn't like? Never said, "How late does the buffet line stay open?" Never said "No" to a doggy bag? What?

MABEL
So, what are you saying?

MAXINE
I'm saying, yes. Your jogging suit makes your butt look big.

MABEL
(*Adjusting her breasts.*) I kinda thought wearing this push-up bra might offset that.

MAXINE
Only if you sewed tassels to it. And, even then, they'd hafta be the size of chandeliers to offset what you got back there--

MABEL
How long have I known you? How long?

MAXINE
I'm not sure. Maybe thirty years?

MABEL
And, every month I come in here, plunk down my money--

MAXINE
If you have less than a hundred--

MABEL
And, listen to your insults.

MAXINE
Consider it a cover charge for the entertainment. (*She laughs. So does MABEL.*)

>   *MABEL and MAXINE continue to talk quietly and exercise. LIGHTS dim on them. LIGHTS up on JANE and RONNIE.*

JANE
Is Maxine happy?

RONNIE
What do you mean?

JANE
Just that. Does she look happy to you?

RONNIE
She's funny sometimes. And, she's always teasing with Mabel.

JANE
Maybe it's because she's not…you know.

RONNIE
She's not what?

JANE
I dunno. I mean, you know, she's not very feminine. She kinda walks like a wrestler. Haven't you noticed that? Please, please don't get me wrong. I really like her, but…

RONNIE
Well, maybe she grew up with a lot of brothers. Maybe on a farm, or something. Not much chance of becoming a lady in a situation like that. Maybe her father was really hard on her, and--

JANE
Maybe. I really do like her, though. (*Wistful*) She seems very confidant. I wish that I could….

RONNIE
Could what?

JANE
Be, you know, confidant. Feel that just once--

RONNIE
Come on. Didn't your high school students get second place in the whole state last year? We never went that far. Weren't you runner-up for teacher of the year two years in a row? I know you were the year I graduated.

JANE
I just had some terrific students like you, that's all, they made me look good.

RONNIE
Come on, Jane. Your kids love you, don't you know that?

JANE
(*Smiles*) They're good kids. Usually. (*Looks at clock*) I have to get to school early today by 7. I promised to meet some of them for an extra credit project they've got. For once, it's a mix of a couple popular kids and the ones who fly under the radar. (*Pleased at that*)

RONNIE

Under the radar? I know what you mean.

> *Music SOMEONE MUST SEE ME begins softly under following dialogue.*

JANE

Not that they want to, you understand. Believe me I know…sometimes no matter what you do, you just don't get noticed. *(Starts to cry to herself, then sings.)*

SOMEONE MUST SEE ME

SOMEONE MUST SEE ME WHEN NO ONE CAN SEE ME
SOMEONE MUST SEE MY HEART.
WHY CAN'T THEY SEE ME, THOUGH EVERYONE SEES ME
ARE WE ALL MILES APART?

TO SAY I'M NOT NOTICED, TO SAY I'M NOT THERE
AFFIRMS WHAT I'VE ALWAYS KNOWN.
THAT ALL THAT I DO, THAT ALL THAT I SAY
INSURES THAT I'M STILL ALONE.

PLEASE TAKE WHAT I OFFER, OH YES, OH PLEASE DO
ALL THAT I HAVE I WILL GIVE.
AND, IF NOT ALL, THEN PLEASE TAKE A PART
ON THAT I CAN SURELY LIVE.

SAY YOU'LL BE MINE, MY STILL UNKNOWN PRINCE
AND, SAY THAT I'LL BE YOURS TOO.
MY LIFE, MY LOVE, AND ALL THAT I AM
WILL ALL BELONG TO YOU.

JANE

(Music continues under dialogue) I sat behind Rodney Jacobs for four years, but he thought I was a stranger and had crashed his high school graduation party. How embarrassing! Want to hear something even funnier? I got stood up for the prom when Billy Randall asked me to go as a joke. Funny stuff, right?

GIVE ME ONE KISS, OR YOUR HAND, OR A SMILE
DEAR GOD, PLEASE GIVE HIM TO ME.
YES, SOMEONE MUST SEE ME WHEN NO ONE CAN SEE ME
PLEASE LET HIM SEE ME FOR ME.

> *LIGHTS up whole stage.*

MAXINE
(*Noticing from across the room*) Jane? Janie? Are you OK? Are you all right, sweetie?

JANE
(*Quickly wiping tears away*) I'm fine. It's these new eye drops. They kinda--

RONNIE
She'll be fine. Nothing a little workout won't fix. Right Jane? (*JANE doesn't respond*) I said, "Right, Jane?" (*Quietly*) Come on; don't let 'em see you like this. We'll talk later. Besides, we've got a deal.

JANE
(*Recovering*) Oh right. Exercise is my middle name. Because I've got my class reunion and you've got that date with a baby.

RONNIE
(*Whispering to JANE*) Hush on the baby stuff. (*To MAXINE*) She's fine. We're both fine.

MABEL
Well hallelujah, all's right with the Lord. Now Maxine, can you get us some decent music?

MAXINE
I could sing you a bit of *Jesus Loves Me*… (*JANE and RONNIE laugh*)

MABEL
Ronnie, do you have names picked out? If it's a boy, I've always loved the name Roscoe.

MAXINE
Roscoe?

MABEL
I always had a huge crush on Roscoe Karnes.

MAXINE
Who is Roscoe Karnes?

MABEL
I loved him on TV back in the 50s.

MAXINE
No one remembers TV in the 50s, except you.

RONNIE
I'm not naming my child Roscoe. I had a Chihuahua named Roscoe. He was small, wormy, and shook all the time.

MABEL
So did Roscoe Karnes, but I still loved him.

JANE
You could name him after your husband—Troy Chadwick Noonan. The fifth? You could always call him Chad to cut down on the confusion factor.

RONNIE
Yes, that could be a problem. At family reunions, you call for Troy and every man in the place turns his head.

MAXINE
Mabel, you're Baptist, aren't you? You know what they say about Baptists—wherever you find four Baptists, you find a fifth.

MABEL
That's not funny. Well, it is funny but I'm not allowed to laugh at such things. Rev. Calvin wouldn't like it.

MAXINE
Calvin's dead.

MABEL
Don't tell him.

RONNIE
Don't say fifth. That's where Mom gets all her great ideas. (*She mimes drinking.*) But if it's a boy, for sure it'll be another Troy.

JANE
What about girl names?

MABEL
How about Heddy?

RONNIE
Heady? No disrespect, Mabel, but what are you thinking?

MABEL
Heddy Lamar. Wasn't she the most beautiful thing you ever saw?

MAXINE

No one besides Heddy Lamar was ever named Heddy.

MABEL

Heddy Troy Noonan the first.

MAXINE

Mabel, did anyone ever tell you your butt looks big?

JANE

My cat has a toy mouse without the head. (*They look at her, she shrugs*) I found the head buried in her box. I never saw Heddy Lamar. Just trying to make conversation.

RONNIE

(To herself) I got to get pregnant first . . .

MABEL

You can name her Eugenia after my grandmother. She died forty years ago. You've all seen her picture over my mantel.

MAXINE

Yes we did Mabel. Ugliest woman I ever saw. Been buried forty years you say? Probably looks better now.

RONNIE

Enough with the names! Can't we change the subject?

JANE

She's right. Why get all concerned over something that--

RONNIE

Any baby is going to be named whatever Troy's mother says, anyway. You know her. Helen Noonan says it and it becomes "Noonan family law." If I had my way, I'd name it Sissulfuss just to spite her.

MABEL

Sissulfuss Noonan…Do you have a middle name picked out?

MAXINE

Mabel, please.

RONNIE

You've all known her for years. Driving around Kurves, Texas in her big, black Lincoln. Looking down her nose at everyone. Do you know the first thing she ever said to me? Do you? She always uses that awful supercilious tone. *(Mimicking Helen's tone)* "You realize, dear—Veronica, is it?—that Troy has never dated a heavy girl before." (*Starts to cry quietly*) And, Troy just stood there. Finally, he told her that we were going out to dinner, and she looked me up and down. Then she told Troy, "Well, I hope you brought plenty of money."

JANE

Ronnie, please don't—

RONNIE

Me and the town's catch—that was Mom's idea, did I tell you? (*Mimics mom*) "Marry the town prince, the town Adonis, Ronnie, and get set for life." But I really love him, and he loves me, at least I think he does. He just can't stand up to Helen. (*Confessing*) I wasn't pregnant, but I told him I was. (*Ladies look shocked*) Another one of Mom's ideas (*pantomimes taking a shot*). Can you believe we were still in the courtroom when she came up with that. Why did I listen to her? Now I've got to get pregnant. I don't want to lose him!

JANE

Courtroom?

RONNIE

Troy was prosecuting Mom for her second DWI. That's how I met him. *(Sarcastic)* Damn romantic, isn't it? (*(looks at MABEL)* Sorry for the language.

JANE

He loves you. I know he does.

RONNIE

(Angry) How? How do you know? Are you there? Do you see him looking at me like maybe he's made a mistake? You think I don't see him look at other women when he thinks I don't notice?

MAXINE

All guys do that. It's in their nature. All of them have the stupidity gene, and all of them look. They have this brain that shifts from their heads to other places. I hate to say it, but they're just wired to be stupid, sometimes.

MABEL

Well, luckily, women are different. We don't make mistakes…

MAXINE

Right, Mabel. Four husbands is it?

MABEL

Now, I won't listen to that kind of talk. My husbands were all--

MAXINE
Yeah, I know. Comfortable.

MUSIC begins under dialogue.

RONNIE
We're all stupid. Maybe I am more than anyone. *(She sings.)*

THE PICTURE

THERE'S A PICTURE INSIDE MY HEAD
OF THE GIRL I'M SPOZED TO BE.
AND AT NIGHT WHEN I'M IN MY BED
THAT PICTURE SPEAKS TO ME.
THERE'S A BABY THAT WILL MAKE US THREE
HE'S PERFECT! LOOKS JUST LIKE HIS DAD.
THERE'S MY HUSBAND—BUT IT'S PLAIN TO SEE
HE REGRETS I CHANGED THE LIFE HE HAD.
CUZ I DON'T FIT, I'M NOT IN THE PICTURE
I DON'T FIT, I'M OUT OF THE FRAME.
THE WHOLE TOWN KNOWS WE'RE NOT THE RIGHT MIXTURE
BUT I'M JUST CAUGHT UP IN A CINDERELLA GAME.

BUT THE PICTURE THAT'S INSIDE MY HEAD
OF THE GIRL I'M SPOZED TO BE.
WON'T BE SILENT, REPEATS THE WORDS
OF THE LOVE HE PROMISED ME.
SO MY BABY WILL MAKE US THREE
PRESERVE THE LOVE THAT WE SHARE.
AND THAT PICTURE SINGING IN MY HEAD
WON'T BE STILL UNTIL I TAKE THE DARE.

UNTIL I FIT, FIT INTO THE PICTURE
GOT TO FIT, GET INTO THE FRAME.
THE WHOLE TOWN KNOWS WE'RE NOT THE RIGHT MIXTURE
BUT I'M LEARNING HOW TO WIN THIS CINDERELLA GAME.

UNTIL I FIT, FIT INTO THE PICTURE,
GOT TO FIT, GET INTO THE FRAME.
THE WHOLE TOWN KNOWS WE'RE NOT THE RIGHT MIXTURE
BUT I'M LEARNING HOW TO WIN THIS CINDERELLA GAME.

I'M WORKING FOR THE DAY, MY ONE TRUE LOVE WILL STAY
DESPITE THE CHOICE THAT CHANGED THE LIFE HE HAD.

RONNIE
(*Composes herself, begins working out again*) Thanks for listening, I'm okay now. Besides, I need to meet my mother-in-law at 8 this morning, and it takes me a while to get decent. I mean, presentable. She's very particular. Well, she's picky about how I represent the family.

MABEL
I need to get to the soup kitchen by 8:30. It's my day to open.

MAXINE
Get away, Mabel, you open the soup kitchen every day and you know it. And then you close it down, too. (*Grins*) Guess I'm the only one with nobody to meet and nowhere to go. (*Hand thump*) I'll go kick the old 8-track back into gear.

> *MAXINE exits through interior door to hidden back room, WOMEN talk quietly and work out, as BOOTS and FINGERS enter from back of theater, arguing. BOOTS fancies himself a ladies man, and FINGERS is a gentle, simple soul.*

BOOTS
When was the last time you put gas in the car?

FINGERS
I never did.

BOOTS
No wonder we ran out. But the thing runs so rough, gas might not even help. And the filling station in this Podunk town doesn't open for another two hours.

FINGERS
Nothing's open this early. I'm hungry. The hotel over there doesn't even offer free coffee, and you gotta have one of those card thingies to get inside. Do you got money?

BOOTS
Why should I have to always pay? It's your car, your problem. You find the cash.

FINGERS
Okay, then, I will. (*He looks around for likely target*) Hey, there's a car over there. Why don't we just borrow that? Betcha it's got gas and everything.

BOOTS
You got a real eye. That's a classic. 1957 Chevrolet Bel Air, red and white hard top. She'd sure raise some eyebrows—and I need a cool car, but I'm not going to jail for grand theft auto. I gotta get my cool car fair and square, so I can finally settle down.

FINGERS

I just thought . . .

BOOTS

Don't think. Leave the smarts to me. I got it all figured out. Just find us some quick cash for your old clunker. (*He sings*)

PITCHING WOO

(BOOTS)
NEED A CAR TO WOO A LADY
SUAVE DEMEANOR, PERFECT PITCH,
A GIRL WHO RECOGNIZES CHARM,
AND DOESN'T CARE THAT I'M NOT RICH.

NEED SOME CASH TO GAS IT, MAYBE
CRAP APPEARANCE, THERE'S NO HITCH
CLASSIC CARS JUST RAISE ALARM
YOUR OLD RIDE IS JUST MY KITSCH.

(FINGERS)
NEED A FRIEND, I'M NOT A BABY,
DON'T BE MEAN, I'M NOT A SNITCH
WHIRLIND DRIVING MAKES ME QUEASY
MOMMA SAYS IT MAKES ME ITCH.

SEARCHING FOR A SPECIAL LADY
HELPS ME FIND MY PERFECT NICHE
ONE WHO KEEPS ME SAFE FROM HARM
AND WON'T ACT LIKE AN EVIL WITCH.

(BOOTS)
NEED A CAR TO WOO A LADY
SUAVE DEMEANOR, PERFECT PITCH,

(FINGERS)
WHIRLIND DRIVING MAKES ME QUEASY
MOMMA SAYS IT MAKES ME ITCH.

(BOOTS)
NEED SOME CASH TO GAS IT, MAYBE

(FINGERS)
HELPS ME FIND MY PERFECT NICHE.

(BOOTS)
CLASSIC CARS JUST RAISE ALARM, BUT

(FINGERS)
WON'T ACT LIKE AN EVIL WITCH.

(SUNG TOGETHER THREE TIMES as cannon)

(BOOTS)	(FINGERS)
NEED A CAR TO	NEED A FRIEND,
WOO A LADY	I'M NOT A BABY.
SUAVE DEMEANOR,	DON'T BE MEAN,
PERFECT PITCH,	I'M NOT A SNITCH.
A GIRL WHO	WHIRLWIND DRIVING
RECOGNIZES CHARM,	MAKES ME QUEASY
AND DOESN'T CARE	MOMMA SAYS
THAT I'M NOT RICH.	IT MAKES ME ITCH.
NEED SOME CASH	SEARCHING FOR
TO GAS IT, MAYBE	A SPECIAL LADY
CRAP APPEARANCE,	HELPS ME FIND MY
THERE'S NO HITCH	PERFECT NICHE
CLASSIC CARS	ONE WHO KEEPS ME
JUST RAISE ALARM	SAFE FROM HARM
YOUR OLD RIDE IS	AND WON'T ACT LIKE
JUST MY KITSCH.	AN EVIL WITCH.

FINGERS
Hey, that place looks open.

BOOTS
Are you ready? Hey, this should be a piece of cake; it's just a bunch of women.

FINGERS
Cake. That sounds good. *(Inserts finger in pocket to simulate gun.)*

BOOTS
(Opening the door) Okay ladies, this is a stick-up! *(To MABEL, slides up to her, says slyly)* Or should I say, pick up? *(He leers)*

EVERYONE reacts. MABEL is not amused, others shocked.

FINGERS
Don't move. Freeze. Stand still. This thing's loaded and I'm not afraid to use it. I got you covered. I got an itchy finger…I mean trigger finger. Aw c'mon, will ya freeze already?

BOOTS
(Checking cash register) It's empty! There's nothing.

MABEL
Welcome to Maxine's.

BOOTS
(To MABEL) What's your sign?

MABEL
I'm not into that zodiac witch-craftery mumbo jumbo, sonny. And don't point that thing at me!

BOOTS
(To others) What are your signs?

JANE
It's going to be one of those days.

MAXINE enters from back room.

MAXINE
I can't get the damn 8-track to work . . . what's going here? Excuse me, gentlemen, this is ladies only.

BOOTS
Well helloooo…and what's YOUR sign?

JANE
They said it's a stick up. But we don't know what they want. Something about the zodiac. Maybe you better tell him your sign, Maxine.

MAXINE
I'm going to kill you, that's my sign. Seriously, you need to leave.

BOOTS
Oh, I like 'em rough!

FINGERS
Will you quit fooling around, Boots. We need money for gas.

BOOTS
(*To Maxine*) If you're going to stab me, stab me with love.

FINGERS
(*To Ronnie and Jane*) Do those lines work anymore?

JANE
Those are lines? (*Aside to RONNIE*) He's sort of cute.

FINGERS
(*To Boots*) Remember what we're here for.

BOOTS
(*To everyone*) I hope you don't think I'm like this with all the girls. Who's in charge here? (*The ladies point at MAXINE*) Where do you keep your rope?

MAXINE
I don't have any rope, but if I did, I'm at the end of mine.

BOOTS
Then where do you keep your string?

MAXINE
We don't have any string.

BOOTS
Where do you keep your tape?

MAXINE
In the back. I'll get it.

MABEL
(*Grabs his arm*) Don't help them!

MAXINE
(*Aside to her*) Play along. Stall for time, tell a story. Blow some smoke of your own, will you? Keep 'em off balance.

FINGERS
(*Overhearing, and whispering back*) But I don't smoke—even secondhand makes me cough.

BOOTS
Quit whispering. Fingers, take her to get the tape.

MAXINE exits to get tape, FINGERS follows. Sounds of an offstage scuffle. MAXINE returns rubbing her arms. FINGERS follows with sparkly Christmas ribbon.

FINGERS
She just wanted to escape out the back door. (*To MAXINE*) Are you okay? I didn't mean to hurt you. But sneaking away isn't in the plan. (*Hands BOOTS fancy ribbon*) I couldn't find any tape.

BOOTS and FINGERS tie everyone up with ribbon, elastic bandage, jump ropes and search each person for valuables.

BOOTS
(*To MAXINE*) We'll start with you, big girl. Empty your pockets.

MAXINE
Believe it or not, these designer togs came pocket-free. Go figure.

BOOTS
No jewelry? What about a watch?

MAXINE
That clock on the wall has worked fine for 30 years.

BOOTS
Car keys? (*Puts MAXINE into rolling desk chair*)

MAXINE
I walk to work. How do you think I keep this trim figure?

BOOTS
(*To FINGERS*) She's clean. (*To MAXINE*) Give me a kind word and I'll live on it forever.

MAXINE
The word is, I'm still going to kill you.

BOOTS
(*To RONNIE*) What about you? Got anything? Jewelry? Keys?

RONNIE
(*Covers wedding rings*) My husband dropped me off, and my mother-in-law will pick me up. You can't have these; they're family heirlooms, for three generations.

BOOTS
Hand 'em over. They've got a new family now.

RONNIE
(*Does so, weeping*) Troy will kill me. His mother will kill me. I'm dead.

BOOTS
(*To RONNIE, as he ties her to exercise equipment*) Don't cry, you make my eyes sing, sweetheart. (*Moves to MABEL, holds her hands to tie them*) If I can hold your hand for only a moment, then it's better than holding the world's gold for all eternity. (*Tries to take her ring*)

MABEL
(*Slaps hands away*) You can have the ring, I got four more sets. But you struck out on the car again, bucko. Your name's not Roscoe is it?

FINGERS
His name's Danny Blootman.

BOOTS
Don't tell them my name, you dummy!

FINGERS
Sorry, Boots. She asked nice. I was just being polite.

BOOTS
(*Looks at JANE—she holds out her hands to be tied*) I can see you got nothing. (*Walks away. JANE is crushed.*)

FINGERS
(*Sees Jane's reaction*) I'll do it. (*Asks JANE quietly*) Do you have a car? (*JANE nods—but FINGERS puts his fingers to lips and pantomimes locking lips. To BOOTS, in his best "gangster" voice*) Do we have enough? What's the haul? (*To everyone*) I've always wanted to say that!

BOOTS
Plumb pitiful. Some jewelry but no way to pawn it. No car. Now what?

FINGERS
This is just like <u>Purple Heart</u>. You know, where all the POWs were tied up?

MABEL
I saw that. Dana Andrews, Farley Granger, that was a great movie. But it's nothing like this.

FINGERS
It's exactly the same…only different. Hey, did you ever see <u>The Man Who Knew Too Much</u>?

MABEL
Jimmy Stewart, Doris Day, do you remember the part where they—

MAXINE
Mabel? (*He cuts eyes at the phone on the desk, and scoots the rolling chair that direction*) Sure wish I had me a smoke. (*She looks puzzled, and he tries again*) A smoke would sure be good about now. Smoking smokity smoke, how I love to BLOW SMOKE. (*He cuts eyes at phone again. MABEL finally understands but looks panicked*)

FINGERS
(*To MAXINE*) Smoking's bad for you. (*To MABEL*) Hey, so you really have four sets of wedding rings? I mean, you said—

MABEL
(*Distracted*) Honey, before I met Reverend Calvin, I thought I was going to have a set for every finger on both hands.

FINGERS
I don't get it.

MAXINE
(*Rolls a bit closer to the phone, runs into BOOTS*) Got a smoke? (*BOOTS moves away from desk*)

MABEL
(*A "eureka" look*) Well, my first husband, Myrtt was…well, we were very young. And, we were very much in love. He wasn't all that nice sometimes, but you overlook a lot when you're in love. We eloped. We saved everything we could and bought this little house, but Myrtt died. He caught pneumonia. I lost the house after that, and I was alone for a while until Newton came along. Newton was older. And he was dashing, so very dashing. (*Wistfully, dreamily*) Our children would have been beautiful—two boys, three girls (*interrupts herself from that lost dream*) I remember he had this tall reddish-brown horse that we both just loved.

> *As MABEL continues everyone is riveted except MAXINE who scoots rolling chair closer and closer to desk phone.*

FINGERS
What happened to Norton?

MABEL
Newton! Oh, the horse threw him. He hit hard on this rock, and—

FINGERS

The horse hit his head?

MABEL

No! Norton…I mean, Newton hit his head on the rock. The poor man suffered for days, then…Well, I gave the horse away. Newton had a lovely funeral, though. Everyone came. Then I met Jorje'. Jorje' Milton Belew. I guess it was too soon to get married. He was a sweet man, but we didn't have much in common. But, he sang beautifully. He loved to work in his shop, and he would sing Negro spirituals. Oh, to hear him sing "Swing Low Sweet Chariot" was just…well, it would make me swoon. Literally swoon. Jorje' was killed by a teenage driver. The young man was going to pick up his date, and ran over poor Jorje' while he was walking home from the store.

FINGERS

I feel sorry for both of them.

MABEL

Then I married Reverend Calvin. He was a widower who presided over Newton's as well as Jorje's funerals. He was a kind man who had a little money--

MAXINE

A LOT of money. *(She's now very close to having the phone ready to dial)* And as I recall, he smoked. Really slooooooow . . .

MABEL

(She nods understanding) Anyway, and he was the one who loved movies. We'd see every movie that came out. We'd go to the picture show every time it changed. We saw them all, and we'd watch them on TV, too. My goodness, how we loved the movies! We had many, many wonderful years, Calvin and I. He went to sleep one afternoon, and he just never woke up. And, do you know what that silly man was buried with?

FINGERS

What?

MABEL

It was in his will that he wanted to be buried with his autographed picture of Gale Storm.

MAXINE knocks the phone off the desk.

BOOTS

You calling for a hot date or something? *(He crosses to the desk, picks up scissors and cuts the phone cord)* I don't have a date, nobody has a date. And there's not enough here for a tank of gas, let alone a cool car! There's no way to catch the eye of that perfect babe without a cool car. *(He sings/dances)*

YOU'RE THE CHICK FOR ME!

HEY, THERE, BE MY BABY.
PLEASE SAY 'YES' OR MAYBE, 'MAYBE.'
I'M NOT THIS WAY WITH ALL THE GIRLS.
SOMEHOW, WITH YOU IT'S DIFFERENT.
MARRY ME, WE'LL RAISE AN INFANT.
A CUTIE LIKE YOU, WITH LOTSA CURLS.

(jazzy talking) D'YA PLAY THE PIANO? BECHA DO.
MAKE YOUR OWN CLOTHES? I KNOW IT'S TRUE.
ALL THE GIRLS LIKE YOU, THROUGH AND THROUGH.
(sings) YOU'RE THE CHICK FOR ME!

WHAT'S YOUR SIGN? I'M A LIBRA.
DO YOU LIKE PETS? WE'LL BUY A ZEBRA.
THE SUN IS CAPTURED IN YOUR HAIR.
YOU OWN MY HEART, NOW OWN MY LIFE.
JUST SAY "YES, I'LL BE YOUR WIFE."
YOU'RE THE BLUE RIBBON AT THE COUNTY FAIR.

(Jazzy talk) YOU'RE THE SALSA ON MY ENCHILADA.
PRETTY HOT, COULDN'T GET MUCH HOTTA.
A REAL SLICK BABE, A REAL TOMATA
(sings) YOU'RE THE CHICK FOR ME.

DANCE BREAK

YOU'RE THE CHICK FOR ME.
LIKE ELMER'S SAYS, "I'M STUCK ON YOU."
STICK TO ME, WE'LL MAKE IT THROUGH.
BONDED TIGHT ALL THROUGH THE NIGHT.
MY FLAME FOR CHICKS BURNS LIKE A ZIPPO.
I LIKE 'EM THIN. I LIKE 'EM HIPPO.
LOOK FOR MY HEART BOTH DAY AND NIGHT.

(Jazzy talk) YOU JUST MAKE MY EYES SING REAL DANG LOUD.
YOU SURE STAND OUT IN A CROWD.
I CAN'T SEE THE SKY, CUZ YOU'RE MY CLOUD.
YOU'RE THE CHICK FOR ME.
(sings) YES…YOU'RE THE CHICK FOR ME!!!

MAXINE
You think that's all it takes?

BOOTS
Well, not all it takes. But a great car will sure grease the skids, so to speak.

MAXINE
You haven't even started to figure out life.

FINGERS
And you have?

MAXINE
How many times you been married Mabel? How many times before you got it right? It was four, am I right?

MABEL
Were you even listening? I told you I don't do smoke. The last one was a keeper. If his heart hadn't given out.

MAXINE
What about you Ronnie? Is marrying the town prince the happily-ever-after you expected? You want to tell us about his family?

JANE
What about you Maxine? You're the mystery woman of the whole town. If you've got it all figured out, please share with the rest of us.

CURVES

(MAXINE)
I MADE MY PLANS, WITH MY ONE TRUE LOVE,
MAPPED EVERY STEP TO BE,
GRABBED LIFE WITH BOTH HANDS, FOR MY ONE TRUE LOVE,
NO ROLLING THE DICE FOR ME.
BUT I STUMBLED AND FELL, THOUGH MY ONE TRUE LOVE
DIDN'T KNOW I'D LOST MY WAY,
AND I WENT TO HELL WHEN MY ONE TRUE LOVE
DIDN'T KNOW THE DEBTS I'D PAY.

(CHORUS)
CURVES, WHEN THE ROAD SEEM STRAIGHTEST THERE'LL BE
CURVES, WHEN THE PATH SEEMS SAFEST THERE'LL BE
CURVES, WHEN YOUR PERFECT PLAN UNFURLS THE
CURVES WILL THROW YOU.

NERVES, WON'T HELP THE ROAD GET STRAIGHTER
SWERVES, DON'T HELP THE PATH TURN SAFER
NO ONE DESERVES TO LIVE WITH CURVES.

THIRTY YEARS HAVE PASSED SINCE MY ONE TRUE LOVE
AND TODAY I WEAR A MASK.
I HIDE THE PAIN OF MY ONE TRUE LOVE
AND NEVER AGAIN WILL ASK—
TO RISK MY HEART FOR ANOTHER LOVE
OR PLAN BEYOND TODAY.
CURVES COST ME DEAR AND LOST MY ONE TRUE LOVE
IT'S A PRICE TOO HIGH TO PAY.

(CHORUS, repeat)

FINGERS
(To JANE) I hope your life hasn't been a hat full of rain.

> *During song CELIA enters from back of theater. She wears sparkly workout clothes, jewelry, makeup and hair perfect.*

CELIA
(Opens door into BOOTS, knocks him aside.) Sorry…are you open?

FINGERS
Wow. You're shiny!

> *FINGERS drops lunchbox, which falls open and all contents spills out. JANE uses taped hands to help him gather treasures and put back inside box.*

FINGERS
Don't touch my stuff! Nobody touches my lunchbox.

BOOTS
Where the hell did you come from?

MABEL
Watch your mouth, Danny whatsis. My cat buries stuff cleaner than that.

FINGERS
(To Jane) I had a cat once. His name was Rhet Butler.

BOOTS
Hey you, Maxine. Where are the keys to this joint? (*MAXINE indicates ring of keys hung on coat rack, and BOOTS locks the door.*)

CELIA
I walked over from the hotel. The front desk said you provide the workout equipment for guests. (*Notices people tied up.*) What's going on? (*Starts to grin.*) Am I being punk'd? Is this Candid Camera?

BOOTS
The key broke. Son of a—(*Stops when Mabel glares. Notices CELIA*) Wow. If you're going to stab me, stab me with your love.

MABEL
You've already used that one.

BOOTS
Oh. (*Waits a beat*) The flame I feel for you burns brighter than any zippo. (*Turns to the crowd for approval*) There's a hole in my chest where you stole my heart?
EVERYONE but CELIA looks at each other and then applauds with tied hands.

CELIA
Did I walk into something strange here? Did my manager put you up to this?

FINGERS
You got to get her jewels, Boots. That's a lot of gas money she's wearing.

MABEL
You broke the key? So what's the plan for your <u>Great Escape</u>?

FINGERS
Steve McQueen, James Garner, Donald Pleasance, Richard Attenburrough, David McCallum, Charles Bronson, James Coburn, James Donaldson

JANE
I actually saw that one.

FINGERS smiles at JANE, rifles through lunch box and shows her the ticket stub from that movie.

BOOTS
Quit playing around, Fingers, and tape her up and frisk her. With all that hardware she's sure to have some folding money. I want to get out of here.

MABEL
We all of us have places to be, you know. People will miss us, and come looking.

JANE
(Quietly) Some of us will be missed.

FINGERS takes CELIA'S jewelry, deposits in the lunch box.

CELIA
I've got a plane to catch. The hotel shuttle leaves at 8. I left my money in the room— why don't you let me go get it--

BOOTS
Nice try. We'll just sit tight until the pawn shops open.

MAXINE
Yep. And then you can say OPEN SESAME for the door to swing wide, too.

CELIA
Did I land in the middle of a Three Stooges movie?

FINGERS
Moe Howard, Larry Fine, Shimp Howard, Curly Howard, Joe Derita, and Joe Besser. Classic.

JANE
(To CELIA) You look familiar.

CELIA
I get that a lot.

JANE
No, wait! I know you. I mean, I've seen you on TV. Celia Lovejoy! You're that motivational speaker, changed the lives of men and woman all over. I watched your show forever, and I've got your tape BE A SELF-MADE YOU. I listen every day.

CELIA
How's that working for you?

FINGERS
Good, right? Right?

CELIA
(To FINGERS) Are you for real?

FINGERS
Yes.

CELIA
I've got a seminar in Dallas this afternoon, with 7500 people coming. You could say I'm motivated to get out of here on time.

FINGERS
(*To CELIA*) Wow, you're on TV? You know any of the big stars?

CELIA
I know them all.

FINGERS
Did you know Pat Brady? Gale Davis? Or Gene Autry? Did you know Jimmy Hawkins? Rusty Hamer? Or Don Knots?

CELIA
I met Don Knots once. He was kind of small, wormy and shook all the time.

MABEL
There's a lot of that going around.

MAXINE
I'll need to see your room key.

CELIA
Seriously? (*FINGERS busy tieing her up, digs in CELIA's pocket, shows the key card*) So now I have your permission to exercise? (*Gestures with taped hands*) What do I do, hop in place? Is this men's exercise day, and what's with the tape?

MABEL
It skips.

CELIA
Beats hopping.

FINGERS
I like the bunny hop.

CELIA
I am in the Twilight Zone!

FINGERS
Do you hokey pokey, too?

BOOTS
Shut up everyone, I got to concentrate! Make a plan.

FINGERS
What's the plan again?

JANE
(*To CELIA*) It's a hold up. They're robbing us.

RONNIE
They took my wedding rings. I'm in so much trouble.

BOOTS
Fingers, get over here, they're not going anywhere. (*To the ladies*) Talk among yourselves. You too, Maxine.

> *BOOTS and FINGERS cross to one side of stage to confer.*

FINGERS
I don't know what we're supposed to do right now.

BOOTS
What about the back door?

FINGERS
Oh, good idea! You really do have brains.

BOOTS
(*To LADIES*) And the looks to go with them!

> *FINGERS and BOOTS exit into back room*

MABEL
(*To MAXINE*) I'm not paying for this session.

CELIA
The hotel manager will get my complaints, believe me! This is not the service I'm accustomed to.

> *LADIES easily remove their own and each other's tape.*

MABEL
We out number them.

MAXINE
They can't get the back door open. It's been locked since I bought the place. We can rush them when they come back out. (*Does the hand thump*)

CELIA
What did you just do?

MAXINE
I said we can rush them when they come out.

CELIA
No, that thing with your hands.

MAXINE
I'm sorry, it's just a habit.

CELIA
Never mind, it just reminded me of something. *(Looks puzzled)*.

JANE
You really have helped me.

CELIA
That's good to know.

RONNIE
Just what is it that you do? *(To Jane)* She helped you? Could she help me, do you think?

MABEL
Everybody could use some help. Some more than others.

CELIA
That's my business, helping people help themselves. And I get paid very well for it.

RONNIE
I've been trying to help myself. It's not working out very well.

DREAMS FOR SALE

(CELIA)
IF I CAN DO IT YOU CAN DO IT TOO, I'M A SELF MADE ME!
IF I CAN SEE IT YOU CAN BE IT, JUST LIKE ME!
TIRED OF SPINNING YOUR WHEELS
WHEN EVERYONE ELSE IS WINNING SWEET DEALS
(spoken) I CAN FIX THAT!

DREAMS FOR SALE, I'VE GOT DREAMS FOR SALE.
GET THEM WHILE THEY'RE FRESH.
DON'T LET WHAT OTHERS SAY RULE YOUR DAY.
I'VE GOT THE SECRET TO SUCCESS.

DREAMS FOR SALE, GET YOUR DREAMS ON SALE.
SWEEP OUT THE DON'TS, THE WON'TS AND CAN'TS
JUST TAKE MY WORDS TO HEART, AND GRAB A FRESH NEW START
FOR YOUR SAKE JUST TAKE A CHANCE.

(RONNIE & JANE)
WOW, YOU DID IT, CAN'T BELIEVE IT'S TRUE

(CELIA) I'M A SELF MADE ME.

(RONNIE & JANE)
NOW I SEE IT…CAN'T STAND IT…BEING ME!
WE'RE TIRED OF SPINNING OUR WHEELS
WHEN EVERYONE ELSE SEEMS SO MUCH MORE REAL.

(CELIA-*spoken*) I CAN FIX THAT!

(CELIA, RONNIE, JANE)
DREAMS FOR SALE, DREAMS FOR SALE
I (YOU) GRABBED AND CAUGHT THE BRASS RING
EVERY DAY, THINGS JUST GO MY(YOUR) WAY

(CELIA)
THIS WORK-A-HOLIC HAS—EVERYTHING.

(CELIA, RONNIE, JANE)
DREAMS FOR SALE, DREAMS FOR SALE
TAKE A CHANCE, WHAT COULD GO WRONG?

(CELIA)
JUST TAKE MY WORDS TO HEART, GRAB A FRESH NEW START

(CELIA, RONNIE, JANE)
AND FIND WHERE YOU BELONG.

                         RONNIE
Wow, maybe I CAN do it!

                         CELIA
(*Still in salesman mode*) Of course you can! Just look at me. (*continues singing*)

I WAS POOR, LIFE SLAMMED THE DOOR ON LOVE.
SO I PICKED THE LOCKS!
HAD TO REINVENT MYSELF,
THINK OUTSIDE THE BOX.

Slower, introspective.

BUT I'M TIRED OF SPINNING GREAT DEALS
WHEN EVERYONE ELSE SEEMS SO MUCH MORE REAL.
(*spoken*) I CAN'T FIX THAT.

DREAMS FOR SALE. DREAMS FOR SALE.
I GRABBED AND CAUGHT THE BRASS RING.
EVERY DAY THINGS JUST GO MY WAY.
HOW'D THIS WORK-A-HOLIC GET HER EVERYTHING?
DREAMS FOR SALE. DREAMS FOR SALE.
I'M SATISFIED, WHAT COULD BE WRONG?
I'M NOT AFRAID OF THE CHOICE I MADE.
(*to RONNIE and JANE*) I'M RIGHT WHERE I BELONG.

CELIA
I'm from a small neighborhood in Queens. I had nothing growing up. Oh, I had some plans early on but life threw me a curve and—like they say—I made lemonade.

MABEL
Got to add enough sugar or lemonade sucks. (*EVERYONE looks at her*) Voice of experience. I had my ups and downs and downs and downs. (*She's not impressed with CELIA*) Lemonade doesn't taste all that good after a while.

CELIA
(*A bit shaken by MABEL's comment*) Maybe you didn't have the right recipe. Mine tastes just fine!

MABEL
Have you tried prune juice?

JANE
(*To Ronnie*) You're going in the right direction. Just have a little faith in the plan. After all, you've got the baby to think about.

CELIA
I've got to get out of here. Tweedle Dum and Dummer won't be in there forever.

MAXINE
I don't know about that.

Noises from back room of frustration from BOOTS and FINGERS. WOMEN wait at the door for them to exit.

BOOTS
(From offstage) The door wouldn't budge!

FINGERS
You didn't have to hit it with my lunchbox. NEVER touch my lunchbox!

The pair appears in doorway. FINGERS clutches lunchbox protectively to chest. MABEL grabs him by ear and puts in rolling desk chair while MAXINE ties hands. FINGERS sees the ring on ribbon around her neck. Other ladies grab BOOTS and shuffle him to other side of stage and tie him up. LIGHTS dim on them.

FINGERS
You hid that ring from me, I ask nice and you hid it. Wait. *(He looks closer)* That looks like one I seen before. *(MAXINE makes a motion to hide the ring and FINGERS dodges as though expecting a blow.)* Please don't hurt my lunchbox—

MAXINE
The ring means nothing. It's a cheap—I mean, inexpensive ring. It wouldn't do you any good. You couldn't get anything for it.

FINGERS
No, but I've seen that before. I remember sparkly stuff, and that's really sparkly.

MAXINE
It doesn't matter. It doesn't mean a thing to anyone but me. *(Looks toward CELIA)*

FINGERS
I knew this guy in jail once—

MAXINE
You were in jail? For what?

FINGERS
Did you ever have a sister?

MAXINE
I had a family. Once. But that was a long time ago.

FINGERS

My sister wanted to go to the prom. We never had money, not for stuff like that. Or anything nice, really. There was this grocery store. The dress my sister wanted was $35. It was so beautiful, it matched her eyes. I put a paper bag over my head, punched out two holes for the eyes, and asked the checkout girl for $35. That's all I needed. I just wanted to see my sister smile for once. I gave my sister the money and she got the dress.

MAXINE

So how did they catch you?

FINGERS

She looked prettier and happier than I'd ever seen her look.

MAXINE

Again, how'd they catch you?

FINGERS

On the way out, I dropped my lucky rabbit's foot. It was pink, and I carried it everywhere. I lost my luck that day. Even in jail, that was the happiest six month of my life—it was worth it, just seeing my sister's face. I'm going to show you something but you've got to promise not to laugh. People laugh at me a lot. (*He opens lunch box, takes out a picture and shows it to MAXINE.*) My sister in the prom dress.

MAXINE

She really is beautiful.

FINGERS

(Beams) I know where I've seen that ring before. The guy I met in jail wore it on his pinkie. It was real special to him, too.

> *LIGHTS dim on MAXINE and FINGERS, as LIGHTS UP on other side of stage, MABEL is manhandling BOOTS and he's enjoying it.*

BOOTS

You missed a spot. *(He wiggles toes and one of the ladies tapes his feet together)*

MABEL

I'm going to beat you black and blue in every spot.

BOOTS

You're beautiful when you're angry.

MABEL

I give up. There's nothing you can do or say to him that fazes him.

JANE

But he is sort of cute.

BOOTS

Back atcha honey.

JANE

(Giggles)

CELIA

Now somebody call the police. I left my cell phone at the hotel.

RONNIE

So did I. I mean, mine's at home.

CELIA

What about that one on the desk? This is a business isn't it? Surely they have a phone.

RONNIE

The robbers cut the phone line.

CELIA

It just gets better and better! At least I got my workout. It's hot in here. *(She takes off her sparkly jacket, and a ribbon around her neck is seen).*

RONNIE

What's that?

CELIA

What? Oh, that? *(Pulls out the ribbon and a sparkly ring, the twin of MAXINE's is seen)* It's nothing. Just a memory from a long time ago.

(LIGHTS up on whole stage)

BOOTS

(To Celia) You want to go out for coffee after all this is over?

CELIA

(Ignores him)

BOOTS

(To Mabel) What about you big girl? Dinner and dancing? There's a reason they call me Boots.

MABEL

I'm going to kill you.

BOOTS
(*To Maxine*) You're kind of rough, but I like 'em rough. Salad and tea?

MAXINE
Only if you buy.

BOOTS
(*Excitedly*) Really?

MAXINE
I'm going to kill you.

BOOTS
(*To Jane*) Should I even ask? I know you're out of my league . . .

JANE
(*startled and flattered*) Really?

BOOTS
Give me a yes and I can live on the dream

JANE
That's so romantic! (*They look at each other, sparks fly*)

MABEL
(*To Maxine*) Hold me back, now I'm going to kill him!

CELIA
Well, I want my stuff back. (*Goes to Fingers and tries to take lunch box. He fights her for it.*) I only want what's mine. I won't touch your stuff.

FINGERS
Promise? Cross your heart? It's old stuff, but it's special. It's all I got. No one but my mommy ever touched this. No one.

CELIA
(*Taken aback*) Cross my heart.

CELIA opens box, takes one thing out at a time, as FINGERS describes each object—what it means.

FINGERS
Well…That's a movie ticket to Old Yeller. And that one's to Dumbo. The elephant, not the person. And that's to Heidi; I always wanted a grandpa like that.

CELIA holds up picture.

MAXINE
That's his sister, in the most beautiful dress in the world.

CELIA holds up a piece of paper.

FINGERS
I got a C on that book report. My teacher didn't count off for spelling that time.

CELIA
(*Holds up old watch band with shoe string*) What's this?

FINGERS
That's a collar I made for Banjo, the bestest dog I never had.

CELIA
(*Holds up wedding rings*) Two pairs of wedding rings?

MABEL
Mine. And hers. (*Points to RONNIE, who happily collects and puts on rings.*)

CELIA
And all my sparkles. (*Starts putting on jewelry*)

FINGERS
Oh look, you've got a sparkly ring around your neck, too. (*To MAXINE*) See I told you I'd seen it before.

MAXINE, turned away, does hand thump. CELIA finally recognizes MAX shows several emotions—surprise, shock, joy and finally anger and hurt. MUSIC starts playing, a calliope mocking sound.

CELIA
This explains a lot. (*Adjusting jewelry, and hurt and seething*).

JANE
I love your jewelry, Celia. And I love what you're doing with your life. I always wanted to be the girl with the sparkles.

LIFE HAPPENS

(JANE & CELIA verse 1.)
I WANT (GET) TO BE THE GIRL WITH THE SPARKLES
I WANT (GET) TO SEE THE VIEW FROM THE TOP
TAKE MY PLACE, MAKE MY MARK.
DESTINY YOU CAN'T STOP.

(MABEL & RONNIE verse 2.)
I SEE MYSELF SWEET AND SO DEMURE
WON'T LET THIS WEALTH BE MY CURE
CAN'T LOSE MY PLACE, IT'S NOT FAIR!
I DON'T HAVE TIME TO SPARE
DESTINY YOU WON'T STOP.

(MAXINE—CHORUS)
LIFE HAPPENS, LIFE HAPPENS
LIFE HAPPENS THAT WAY
FORGET YOUR INTENTIONS,
YOUR BEST INTERVENTIONS
GET KICKED TO THE CURB EVERY DAY.

(BOOTS & FINGERS verse 3.)
YOU'VE GOT IT GOOD, WHY CAN'T YOU SEE
JUST WISH I COULD, MAKE IT BE ME.
TRADE MY PLACE, OR I'LL SHARE
WHY WON'T SOMEBODY CARE
DESTINY I WANT TO STOP.

Verses combined, sung twice in harmony, then . . .

(MAXINE--CHORUS)	(CELIA--DESCANT)
LIFE HAPPENS,	LIFE WITHOUT LOVE HAPPENS,
LIFE HAPPENS	LIFE GOES ON, IT HAPPENS
LIFE HAPPENS THAT WAY	LIFE SOMETIMES HAPPENS THAT WAY
FORGET YOUR INTENTIONS,	FORGET YOU? WOULD NEVER HAPPEN,
YOUR BEST INTERVENTIONS	ALWAYS DREAMED OUR LOVE WOULD LIVE AGAIN
GET KICKED TO THE CURB EVERY DAY.	YET SICK TO MY HEART TODAY.

(MAXINE & ALL--CHORUS)	(CELIA--DESCANT)
LIFE HAPPENS,	LIFE WITHOUT LOVE HAPPENS,
LIFE HAPPENS	LIFE GOES ON, IT HAPPENS
LIFE HAPPENS THAT WAY	LIFE SOMETIMES HAPPENS THAT WAY
FORGET YOUR INTENTIONS,	FORGET YOU? WOULD NEVER HAPPEN,
YOUR BEST INTERVENTIONS	ALWAYS DREAMED OUR LOVE WOULD LIVE AGAIN
GET KICKED TO THE CURB EVERY DAY.	YET SICK TO MY HEART TODAY.

MAXINE removes wig, is revealed as man. All react, LIGHTS OUT.

END ACT I

ACT II

ALL take previous positions during Entre Act instrumental only LIFE HAPPENS, action resumes as though no time elapsed, but lights UP only on CELIA and MAX. MUSIC intro to The Dream begins under dialogue.)

CELIA

Talk about getting kicked to the curb. I've been thrown curves in my life, but nothing like this!

MAX

Celia, I—

CELIA

There's nothing you can say that I want to hear!

CELIA angry, MAX retrospective and tender.

THE DREAM

(CELIA)
WHEN YOU LEFT YOU BANISHED MY TRUST,
AFTER I GAVE YOU MY HEART.
ALL OUR LOVE HAS VANISHED LIKE DUST,
YOU KILLED ME, MY LIFE TORN APART.
NEVER A WORD—ALIVE? OR DEAD?
PROMISED FOREVER WE'D BE WED!
WAS IT SOMETHING I DID, OR SOMETHING I SAID?
A THIRTY-YEAR SILENCE BETRAYS.

--CHORUS

(CELIA)
I HAD A DREAM,
GAVE YOU MY BEST
YOU FILLED UP MY HEART
WITH YOUR LOVE.
AND NOW YOU'RE HERE
IT'S NOT WHAT IT SEEMS
IT'S TIME FOR TRUTH,
TIME TO CONFESS.

(MAX)
I SAW YOU WALK IN,
BUT FOR NOT THE FIRST TIME
WHY IT WAS HERE,
WAS THERE RHYTHM OR
RHYME?
THE YEARS TOUCHED YOU
LIGHTLY,
WERE NEVER UNKIND.
YOU BROUGHT BACK EACH
MEMORY TUCKED AWAY
IN MY MIND, IN MY MIND.

(CELIA)
LOOKED FOR YOU FOR SEVEN LONG YEARS
WONDERED, AND WAITED AND MOURNED.
THEN I FOUND MY SELF-MADE CAREER,
THAT'S HOW SPARKLES WERE BORN
NOTHING TO TRUST WHEN ALL I SEE
EVERYTHING'S FALSE, EVEN SELF-MADE ME
YOUR LOSS CREATED WHAT I CAME TO BE.
CAN'T GO BACK, NOW IT'S TOO LATE.

--CHORUS

(CELIA)
I HAD A DREAM,
GAVE YOU MY BEST
YOU FILLED UP MY HEART
WITH YOUR LOVE.
AND NOW YOU'RE HERE
IT'S NOT WHAT IT SEEMS
IT'S TIME FOR TRUTH,
TIME TO CONFESS.

(MAX)
I WANTED TO TELL YOU
FOR ALL OF THESE YEARS.
I BOUGHT MY SILENCE
WITH THOUSANDS OF TEARS.
TO LOSE YOU, NOW TO SEE
YOU,
REVISITS MY FEARS.
SHOULD I TELL YOU NOW,
LOVE?
I'LL CONFESS IF YOU'LL
LISTEN,
WILL YOU HEAR?

(CELIA)
NOW THAT I SEE YOU, I UNDERSTAND WHY
YOU WANTED ME OUT OF YOUR LIFE
SILENT TEARS ARE MORE THAN A LIE
WHY NOT TELL ME YOU WANTED NO WIFE?
SEEING YOU HERE, BRINGS BACK THE PAST
THE HURT THAT WAS BURIED FOREVER WILL LAST
LOVE WAS A DREAM AWAKENED TOO FAST
DREAMS AREN'T REAL. DREAMS DON'T SURVIVE.
--CHORUS

(CELIA)
I HAD A DREAM,
GAVE YOU MY BEST
YOU FILLED UP MY HEART
WITH YOUR LOVE.
AND NOW YOU'RE HERE
IT'S NOT WHAT IT SEEMS
IT'S TIME FOR TRUTH,
TIME TO CONFESS.

MY LOVE FOR YOU
NEVER WAVERED, IT'S TRUE
BUT I SUPPRESSED IT,
BECOMING MORE BLUE.
I HURT YOU THEN,
BUT I CAN'T HURT YOU ANEW
CALL ME SELFISH, CALL ME MEAN,
BUT I DID IT ALL JUST FOR YOU,
ALL FOR YOU.

(MAX)

LIGHTS UP, everyone reacts that MAXINE is a man.

CELIA

You son-of-a--

MABEL

(*Quickly interrupting*) Peach!

CELIA

What?

MABEL

Son of a "Peach." I'll not listen to any smutty talk, even if we were all thrown on our butts over this development. (*Flustered*) I mean, rear ends. I didn't mean to say butts. You've got me so flustered that I'm saying things that I don't usually say.

CELIA
(To Max) Who are you? What are you? You walked out on me for this? To become this? If you didn't want to marry me, couldn't you just have told me? You had to run out on me, and become a…be a…I don't even know what you are!

FINGERS
He's a man?

BOOTS
Oh, this is perfect. One more man. I'm not big on competition, ya know. I kinda like to work alone.

FINGERS
(To Jane) He's a man!

BOOTS
I thought it was two guys and five babes. Now, it's *(counting on his fingers)*…three guys and four babes. OK, which two of you are gonna be mine?

FINGERS
Right now, I'd say none of them.

CELIA
(To MAX) Do you know what it's like to feel used and tossed aside? Do you? Do you know what it's like to watch a dream vanish, and you don't even know why? Have you ever sat alone, and stared out a window, hoping that the person you loved would come back? Try picking up a phone a hundred times a day, just to see if there's a dial tone, and telling yourself that maybe the phone is broken, and all along you know it's not.

MAX
Celia, please--

CELIA
Please, what? Please understand? Please forgive you? Please don't be upset? Come on, Max, or Maxine, or whatever the hell your name is now!

MABEL
Ahhhh, remember, we don't talk like that.

CELIA
I'll talk any way I want to talk. Who's gonna stop me? You? Any of you? You don't know me, and you sure don't know what I've been through these last thirty years, so don't pretend to censor me because I won't stand for it, from any of you!

JANE
But, you look so…I mean you're so successful. I--

MAX
Stop, Jane. She's right.

CELIA
You bet, I'm right! *(To MAX)* Your parents were murdered. I thought you were at the bottom of a lake somewhere, not playing dress-up in Nowhere, America.

MAX
There's things you don't understand, things I couldn't explain--

CELIA
And, this…this, whatever he is isn't going to be able to say or do anything that'll change how I feel. Just get me out of here. I don't know how, but just get me away from this place and especially him!

RONNIE
You two were in love? And now you've found each other? But that's a fairytale ending! *(Looks around)* What I wouldn't give to have something like that.

JANE
What I wouldn't give to have …anything.

FINGERS
Hey, I know you now. You're the fella from jail. The finger thump guy.

CELIA
Oh yeah, that's what was bothering me. You always did that.

BOOTS
I'll tell you what's bothering me. No car, no date. C'mon chicks, any takers? I'm dyin' here.

FINGERS
What was you doing in jail, anyhow? You never said.

MAX
None of your business.

CELIA
Of course not.

RONNIE
All you do is complain. None of you know how truly lucky you are.

MUSIC intro begins under next lines.

MABEL

Neither do you, Ronnie. None of you have a clue—and it's time to stop your bellyaching. *(MABEL sings waltz tempo/gospel)*

SUCK IT UP SWEETHEART

(MABEL)
SUCK IT UP, SWEETHEART
LUCKS A CROCK, SWEETHEART
WORK IT OUT SWEETHEART
NOTHING COMES FOR FREE
WHEN LIFE'S A BITCH SWEETHEART
AND YOU GOT THE ITCH SWEETHEART
TIME TO MAKE A SWITCH SWEETHEART
JUST REMEMBER ME.
MY DEMEANOR PROTECTS ME JUST FINE.
YOU'LL NOT CRACK THIS HARD SHELL OF MINE.
UNLESS YOU'RE A STRAY, WHO HAS NOW LOST HIS WAY.
THEN NEVER WILL YOU BE ASKING TOO MUCH.

(RONNIE)
IF I'M NOT WORTHY, THEN WHY AM I NOT?
I'M MY GIFT, AND THAT'S ALL THAT I'VE GOT.
AND THROUGHOUT THE YEARS, WHISPER ONCE IN MY EARS
I LOVE YOU. IS THAT ASKING TOO MUCH?

MUSIC continues to vamp under dialogue.

MABEL

No, honey, that's never asking too much. You've just got to hear it when he says it, and he's been saying it for months. It took me three husbands to hear it for real. Just forget what anyone else says or does—you married him, not his mother.

SUCK IT UP, SWEETHEART
LUCKS A CROCK, SWEETHEART
WORK IT OUT SWEETHEART
NOTHING COMES FOR FREE
WHEN LIFE'S A BITCH SWEETHEART
AND YOU GOT THE ITCH SWEETHEART
TIME TO MAKE A SWITCH SWEETHEART
JUST REMEMBER ME.

(FINGERS)
MY DREAM WAS TO ALWAYS BE KIND.
AND THAT OTHERS MIGHT KEEP ME IN MIND.
AFTER ALL OF THESE YEARS, ALL I GOT WAS YOUR JEERS.
KINDNESS MIGHT BE ASKING TOO MUCH.

MUSIC vamp under dialogue.

MABEL
Oh honey, I heard my share of jeers, too, when I lived on the streets after my first husband kicked me out. And you know what I found? True kindness is given, not borrowed or begged. You've got lots of kindness to give, and the folks at the soup kitchen'll lap that up like a bear on honey.

SUCK IT UP, SWEETHEART
LUCKS A CROCK, SWEETHEART
WORK IT OUT SWEETHEART
NOTHING COMES FOR FREE

(FINGERS and MABEL)
WHEN LIFE'S A BITCH SWEETHEART
AND YOU GOT THE ITCH SWEETHEART
TIME TO MAKE A SWITCH SWEETHEART
JUST REMEMBER ME.

MUSIC ends. Audience should believe song is done (wait for applause) Then BOOTS starts his verse when music cues, and we're off and running again.

(BOOTS)
MY DREAM WAS A NEW SHINY CAR.
FROM MY PROBLEMS IT COULD TAKE ME SO FAR.
AFTER ALL OF THESE YEARS, ALL MY HOPES TURNED TO FEARS.
THAT CAR MAY BE ASKING TOO MUCH.

MUSIC ends with flair. Audience should think it's done.

MABEL
What are you thinking? My husband with the Packard was a son-of-a--

FINGERS
Peach?

MABEL

(Smiles) That's right. My last husband drove a Gremlin, and I adored him. Cars, jewels *(looks at RONNIE),* or sparkles *(looks at CELIA)* don't matter in affairs of the heart. When the car drives the man, you're in trouble. And if the car matters to the girl, you're in trouble. Clean off your dirty windshield and you'll see what's waiting right there.

MABEL, FINGERS, RONNIE look at each other, then begin singing in harmony.

SUCK IT UP, SWEETHEART
LUCKS A CROCK, SWEETHEART
WORK IT OUT SWEETHEART
NOTHING COMES FOR FREE
WHEN LIFE'S A BITCH SWEETHEART
AND YOU GOT THE ITCH SWEETHEART
TIME TO MAKE A SWITCH SWEETHEART
JUST REMEMBER ME.

HUGE music finish, applause. A beat, and then...

(JANE)
DO YOU REMEMBER ME AT ALL?
IN SCHOOL WE SHARED THE SAME HALL.
AFTER ALL OF THESE YEARS, SHARING LIFE WITH MY PEERS,
TO NOTICE ME MIGHT BE ASKING TOO MUCH.

MUSIC vamp under next dialogue

MABEL

Just who doesn't notice you, Jane? When I was on the street, I didn't want people to notice me—there's protection in that. It's hard to protect embarrassment. But if you don't reach out, you'll never have a chance to catch that brass ring. The people who matter think you hung the moon—your students, your family, your friends *(indicates those in the room)*. You have to notice yourself to have others see you, too. *(BOOTS and JANE make shy eye contact)*

(MABEL, BOOTS)
SUCK IT UP, SWEETHEART
LUCKS A CROCK, SWEETHEART
WORK IT OUT SWEETHEART
NOTHING COMES FOR FREE

KURVES, THE MUSICAL

(ALL EXCEPT MAX AND CELIA)
WHEN LIFE'S A BITCH SWEETHEART
AND YOU GOT THE ITCH SWEETHEART
TIME TO MAKE A SWITCH SWEETHEART
JUST REMEMBER ME.

A beat. Everyone except CELIA looks pointedly at MAX.

(MAX, with ALL humming harmony backup)
A PENNY BUYS ONE OF MY DREAMS.
A DOLLAR BUYS A HUNDRED IT SEEMS.
AFTER ALL OF THESE YEARS, THEY'RE ALL RUSTED WITH TEARS.
A PENNY MAY BE ASKING TOO MUCH.

MABEL
And I've actually walked into the ladies room with you. Talk about a man of mystery. My family disowned me, never mind why. So I chose a new family—the people at Maxine's, at the soup kitchen—and a true family forgives and loves you no matter what. My dear Rev Calvin taught me that. That's what family does. (*To MAX and CELIA*) And when you find a piece of your lost soul and heart, don't let anything stop you. Not like me. I waited too long and lost it too early.

(ALL except CELIA)
SUCK IT UP, SWEETHEART
LUCKS A CROCK, SWEETHEART
WORK IT OUT SWEETHEART
NOTHING COMES FOR FREE
WHEN LIFE'S A BITCH SWEETHEART
AND YOU GOT THE ITCH SWEETHEART
TIME TO MAKE A SWITCH SWEETHEART
JUST REMEMBER ME.

Everyone looks with expectation at CELIA. She ignores invitation to confess and instead joins MAX SR. for next dialogue with RONNIE eavesdropping. BOOTS and JANE move SL. The two couples aren't aware they echo dialogue on each side of stage. FINGERS and MABEL are UC in dim light.

CELIA
I really don't believe you!

MAX
I never expected this.

CELIA
Didn't you ever consider my feelings for you?

MAX
I can't explain what's going on.

CELIA
I'll tell you exactly what's going on. I show up here, and see you for the very first time.

MAX
I dreamed of this…well, maybe not this way, but I've dreamed of seeing you again.

CELIA
And, this is where we are.

MAX
So, this is what we've got.

BOOTS
(*Hitting on JANE*) I really don't believe you.

JANE
I never expected this.

BOOTS
I have considerable feelings for you.

JANE
I can't explain what's going on.

BOOTS
I'll tell you exactly what's going on. I show up here and see you for the very first time.

JANE
I've dreamed of this. Maybe not this way but I've dreamed of seeing someone like you.

JANE
And, this is where I want to be.

BOOTS
Right now, there's nowhere I'd rather be.

Stage goes dark, spot/area light on CELIA and MAX.

CELIA
There's a lot of places I'd rather be. *(Starts to cross away, MAX stops her)*

MAX
You're going to hear me out! *(Grabs her arm.)*

CELIA
(She looks at him, still angry heartbroken, he let's go.) I've heard and seen more than enough.

MAX
Once upon a time, I loved a woman. But I waited too long to make her mine. There was never enough time, there was never enough money. And I wanted it to be right. And then it all went to hell. Do you understand that?

CELIA
Do you understand I've waited thirty years for an explanation? I'm still waiting.

MAX
I still love you so much, I trust you with my life. And if I tell you, my life is on the line.

CELIA
Give me a break. Still slinging it, you haven't changed.

MAX
You know my folks were killed. Murdered. That's where it begins.

CELIA
I'm sorry. It was in all the papers. But I would have been there for you!

MAX
The police were there for me first. I was the only witness. Do you remember Joey Venitucci.

CELIA
Who? Did you make that name up?

MAX
From the old neighborhood. Joey worked for the mob.

CELIA
You telling me you're in the mob?

MAX
(*Shakes his head no.*) There was a shop owner one block over from my parents' place. He was running numbers. Joey was sent to stop him. One block, that's it. He missed his mark by one block, murdered my parents by mistake. I was coming into the store, and saw the whole thing. Because Joey couldn't read a street map, I saw my family get wiped out. You're all I had left.

Light down on CELIA and MAX. Lights up on BOOTS and JANE.

BOOTS

Repeating your name—Jane, Jane, JANE—will ensure that I'll never be lonely again.

JANE

You don't need a line with me. You are enough.

BOOTS

I'll trade you my life for a moment of your love.

JANE

One moment with you would make my heart sing—(*She sings an arpeggio*)

BOOTS

If my lips touched yours, they've touched heavens.

JANE

I know where the flowers have gone. They're in your eyes.

BOOTS

You own my heart . . .

JANE

(*Beat, she looks at him*) Okay, that's too much even for me. What's your brother think of your lines?

BOOTS

Brother? How do you know my brother? He lives in Cedar Rapids.

JANE

Fingers is not your brother?

BOOTS

Heck, no. He was just asleep in the abandoned car I boosted…I mean, acquired.

LIGHTS DOWN on JANE and BOOTS, LIGHTS UP MABEL and FINGERS upstage center.

PITCHING WOO (Reprise, each sings solo once, and then together as canon)

(FINGERS)	(MABEL)
NEED A FRIEND,	JUST BECAUSE
I'M NOT A BABY,	HE'S NOT A BABY
DON'T BE MEAN,	NEED TO GIVE
I'M NOT A SNITCH	A PERFECT PITCH,
WHIRLIND TALKING	CAN'T BE CHARITY
MAKES ME QUEASY	OR CHEESY,
MOMMA SAYS	HE WON'T CARE
IT MAKES ME TWITCH.	OR SEE I'M RICH.
SEARCHING FOR A	NEED TO FIND A
SPECIAL LADY	SPECIAL AID, HE
HELPS ME FIND	HELPS ME SERVE
MY PERFECT NICHE	MY SPECIAL NICHE
ONE WHO KEEPS ME	ONE WHO KEEPS KIDS
SAFE FROM HARM, AND	SAFE FROM HARM, AND
WON'T ACT LIKE	WON'T THINK I'M
AN EVIL WITCH.	AN EVIL B--PEACH

FINGERS
I can do dishes, I can sweep. I can make coffee. Sorta. If it's instant. I can peel potatoes. I can change a tire. I can rake leaves. I can heat up TV dinners, and I'm real careful turning off stoves. Except for that one time, it was an accident. And I can tell you who starred in every movie ever made. Almost. Rio Bravo—John Wayne, Dean Martin, Walter Brennan, Rickie Nelson. Casa Blanca—Humphrey Bogart--

MABEL
Honey, you don't have to sell yourself to me. I've already bought the package. (*Looks at him.*) And you look to be just fine.

FINGERS
Really? And I got a place to sleep? I mean, not on the floor or anything? I lost my blanket—but I kept my lunch box!

MABEL
I think we've got a bed complete with sheets and blankets and even pillows. We'll find plenty for you to do, you'll fit right in with the regulars.

FINGERS
The regulars? (*Looks worried.*) Will they like me? They won't take my lunchbox, will they?

MABEL
We've got rules against lunchbox thievery. There's a mixed bunch, from motorcycle folks to wannabe gang types.

FINGERS
I can rap! *(Starts to rap, badly—beat box sounds)* My name's Fingers and my car's real nifty, drive real fast, cuz it's really swift-y…

MABEL
That's fine, but I think the regulars take care of their own music. Fingers—wait, I can't call you that. Is that your brother's nickname for you?

FINGERS
He's not my brother, I just hitched a ride with him. I wish he was my brother, he's really smart. My momma called me Willy. *(Shy)* Would you like to see my lunchbox? It's got all my treasures. *(Offers it to her)*.

MABEL
It's very nice to meet you Willy. I'm Mabel. And I'd love to see your lunchbox.

LIGHTS DOWN on MABEL and FINGERS. LIGHTS UP on MAX and CELIA.

MAX
I disappeared all those years ago to protect you. That's how witness protection works.

CELIA
So you're telling me you disappeared all those years ago to protect me? That's the biggest crock I've ever heard. Witness protection, my ass-ets.

MAX
Believe what you want. Because of what I saw, Joey went to prison, and I went to wearing women's clothes.

CELIA
So you're masquerading as a woman to keep the mob from finding you? Listen, honey, your legs aren't that good.

MAX
It's stupid, I know. But after I testified, I had to change everything. I had to move, change my name, my occupation. I had to make a living. This was the only thing available, and the former owner wouldn't sell to a man. So… *(Shrugs)* After a few years, it got easier. It didn't matter that I was the ugliest woman in town. My new friends and Maxine's family didn't care. And I'd already lost the only one I ever wanted to impress.

LIGHTS DOWN on MAX and CELIA. LIGHTS UP on JANE and BOOTS.

BOOTS

I can't believe I told you all that. I've never told anyone that much about me. But you make it really easy to be, well to be real.

JANE

I'm glad. And I still like you. The real you.

BOOTS

I like the real you, too. Because—your eyes are like limpid pools. They keep away all the fools. I know you know all the rules. Because dang it, I love you! (*Smiles*) I just made that up! Enough about me. I heard you're a teacher. What do you teach?

JANE

Poetry.

LIGHTS DOWN on BOOTS and JANE. LIGHTS UP on MABEL and FINGERS.

FINGERS/WILLY

That's lots of stuff to do, for sure. I can help you. I promise I can. You might have to show me once. Well maybe more than once. And sometimes I don't say stuff all el-o-quent-ish, the way educated people do, but I'll do my bestest. (*He sings*)

SILVER SCREEN BLUES

BOGY SAID IT BEST WHEN HE SAID "HERE'S LOOKIN' AT YOU."
NOTHIN' I SAY COMES OUT JUST RIGHT, AND THAT'S WHY I AM BLUE,
YES, I'VE GOT 'EM…THE OL' SILVER SCREEN BLUES.
IF I COULD EXPRESS MYSELF LIKE BOGY, I'D BE TALKIN' TO YOUSE.

HOW DO THE STARS DO IT? MAKE IT ALL COME OUT JUST RIGHT?
I MEMORIZED EVERY SINGLE WORD FROM "THEY DRIVE BY NIGHT."
BUT I'VE STILL GOT 'EM…. THE OL' SILVER SCREEN BLUES.
GEORGE RAFT CAN SAY IT PERFECTLY, STILL I HAVE NO CLUES.

GABLE, COOPER, AND GARFIELD. POWER, MARCH AND DEAN,
ANY PREDICAMENT, HOWEVER BAD, COULD MAKE IT COME OUT CLEAN.
THAT'S WHY I'VE GOT 'EM…THE OL' SILVER SCREEN BLUES.
I'LL COPY THEIR DIALOG WORD FOR WORD, WHAT HAVE I GOT TO LOSE?

SO, "PLAY IT AGAIN SAM", AND "TOMORROW'S ANOTHER DAY."
THAT AND "YOU CAN'T HANDLE THE TRUTH" IS ALL I'VE GOT TO SAY,
CUZ I'VE GOT 'EM…THE OL' SILVER SCREEN BLUES.
IF I WATCH ANOTHER HUNDRED FILMS, THERE'LL BE SOMETHIN' I CAN USE

MAYBE I NEED TO DO IT. START THINKING ON MY OWN,
JUST SAY WHAT IT IS THAT I WANT TO SAY, AND HOPE THE FOLKS DON'T GROAN.
THEN I WON'T HAVE 'EM…THOSE OL' SILVER SCREEN BLUES.
I'LL JUST BE AN ORIGINAL THINKER, WHAT HAVE I GOT TO LOSE?

FINGERS/WILLY

Can I have a job, too? Please? I don't want to just be a do-nothing. Momma always said, charity is okay but you got to do your part.

MABEL

Your lunchbox tells me everything about you.

FINGERS/WILLY

It does? How?

MABEL

Because everything inside lets me know that you recognize what's truly valuable.

FINGERS/WILLY

Wow. That's neato.

MABEL

It sure is. And because of that, I have a job that only somebody with your credentials could do.

FINGERS/WILLY

Credentials? I have credentials? *(Takes lunchbox back and looks inside.)*

MABEL

We have lots of children stay at the shelter and visit the soup kitchen. And they don't have any treasures. They don't even know what to wish for. You'll be in charge of helping them find their own personal treasure that makes them feel special and happy. It won't be easy but I know you can do it. (Beat) Will you take the job?

FINGERS/WILLY

I could do that! *(With excitement, then very poised)* I would be very pleased to accept the job. I'll make you proud. *(They shake hands.)* I've never had a job. What does it pay?

MABEL
(*Taken aback, then smiles.*) What would you accept?

FINGERS
(*Shy again.*) Do you think—could you maybe sometimes hug me? Momma used to.

MABEL
Oh Willy, everyone will love you. And I'll give you an advance on your salary. (*She hugs him.*)

> *Lights down, lights back up on MAX and CELIA. RONNIE approaches, to within hearing distance—the others don't notice.*

CELIA
Thirty years is a long time, Max. Life goes on. I've been married and divorced since then. I can't just pick up where we left off. Even if I wanted to. And I don't.

MAX
To say "I'm sorry" isn't enough, is it?

CELIA
Doesn't even come close.

MAX
You want to talk about it?

CELIA
Not really. What's the use, it won't make any difference now, anyway.

MAX
Nothing that's happened to you could be nearly as bad as what's happened to me.

CELIA
Why you son-of-a…(*Looks around, consciously lowers her voice. It's measured, full of venom, purposely hurtful*). Like I said before, I made myself. Complete with body armor, so I'd never get hurt again the way you hurt me. You even gave me my new name. (*Pulls out ring and reads inscription*) "To the LOVE--JOY of my life." Steven Seidleman, my manager, wanted to be more than that and I tried. Hell, he did everything for me, got me bookings, the TV show, he gave me everything. I owed him. So we got married. He made me me, and I made him miserable. I kept comparing him to you, to this fantasy person who was never real. We lasted seven months. Probably longer than we would have lasted. He's a better manager than husband, and I'm a better "self made me" than a wife. I wasn't meant to be a wife. You did me a favor when you disappeared.

MAX
I did you a favor by not marrying you.

CELIA
We finally agree on something.

MAX
I didn't marry you for all the right reasons. And you married him for all the wrong ones.

CELIA
At least I was there, and told him to his face.

RONNIE
(Interjecting) What is wrong with you people?

CELIA
Stay out of it, this is none of your business.

RONNIE
You think there's a statute of limitations on loving someone?

CELIA
There is in my world.

RONNIE
Then you're in the wrong world. *(To MAX)* You didn't marry for the right reasons before? So what's stopping you now? Do it for the right reasons this time—you don't need to throw it away a second time. *(Looks toward Jane)* High school reunions are full of people who are looking for second chance love, and it never works, because you can't go back in time. Don't you realize that the two of you actually have a chance here? You never had your first chance—so this is your first chance. Don't turn your back on it.

MAX
I'd love to give it a chance, if she wasn't so pig-headed. That at least hasn't changed! It's hard to work with one-sided willingness.

CELIA
You're the one who slammed the door, with that sorry excuse for a reason. At least be a man and own up to--

RONNIE
Stop it! What does the reason matter? *(To MAX)* Do you love her?

MAX
I never stopped.

RONNIE
Celia, did you ever stop loving Max?

CELIA
I made myself stop. I'm in the business of convincing myself and others. I'm very good at it.

MAX
So if you want to, you can convince yourself that we can still work?

CELIA
It's not that easy. Why would I want to?

LIGHTS DOWN on CELIA, RONNIE and MAX.
LIGHTS UP on BOOTS and JANE.

BOOTS
Say what? You teach what?

JANE
I teach poetry.

BOOTS
There was a young man from Nantucket . . .

JANE
Not that kind of poetry. Mine's just a little bit more refined. "A rose by any other name . . ."

BOOTS
…would be a carnation? What? I give up.

POETRY & JAZZ

(JANE)
I'VE PREFER TO READ MY BOOKS, POPULAR WAS NOT IN MY SIGHT.
POETRY MADE UP FOR MY LACK OF LOOKS,
IN MY PRETTY WORLD, I'M A PRETTY GIRL,
IN MY PRETTY WORLD WHERE RHYMES DELIGHT.

(BOOTS) I'M ON MY OWN—ALL ALONE
HUSTLING EACH NICKEL AND DIME.
NOTHING TO OWN—DISCONNECTED PHONE,
BUYING EACH ITEM ON TIME.

(JANE)
EVERY DAY I TEACH A NEW VERSE, POETRY THE LANGUAGE OF LOVE.
BUT ONCE A LONE I CAN'T FEEL MUCH WORSE.
NO ONE CARES FOR ME, I'M ALONE AS CAN BE,
IF SOMEONE CARED, I'D TRADE THE SKY ABOVE.

(BOOTS)
SECONDHAND SUIT, WEEK OLD FRUIT
WORK RECORD NOT WORTH A DAMN.
DRIVING BORROWED CARS, HUSTLING DRINKS IN BARS
THAT'S REALLY WHO I AM.

(JANE)
LONELY IS THE HEART THAT WAITS FOR POETRY TO MAKE THINGS RIGHT.
PERHAPS REFINERY AIN'T MY FATE.
I'LL TAKE A LOOK OUTSIDE, BRAVELY TAKE A RIDE,
IF YOU'RE BY MY SIDE, I'LL TAKE A BITE.
PLEASE GIVE ME JAZZ FOR MY NEW HOOK,
I WANT TO TASTE A NEW FLAVOR TONIGHT.
WE'VE GOT A CHANCE TO REALLY COOK,
SO COME ON, BABY, AND SHOW ME THE LIGHT.

(BOOTS)
REFINEMENT? NOT MUCH. NO CLASS, AND SUCH.
HELP ME BREAK LOOSE IF YOU CAN.
I'M COMMON AS DIRT, FOLKS CALL ME SQUIRT.
WHY CAN'T I BE A GREAT MAN?
I'LL GIVE TO YOU WHAT LITTLE I'VE GOT.
YOU CAN SHARE YOUR SMARTS WITH ME. I'M BEGGING,
I'M HOPING CUZ I'M SURE THIS TIME I'M CAUGHT.
WHAT YOU SEE IN ME, WHAT YOU WANT ME TO BE,
WHAT YOU SEE, IT JUST MIGHT MAKE ME FREE.

(JANE & BOOTS)
PLEASE (I'LL) GIVE ME (YOU) JAZZ FOR A NEW HOOK,
I WANT TO TASTE A NEW FLAVOR TONIGHT.
WE'VE GOT A CHANCE TO REALLY COOK,
SO COME ON, BABY, AND SHOW ME THE LIGHT.

I'LL GIVE TO YOU ALL THAT I'VE GOT,
I (YOU) WILL SHARE MY (YOUR) SMARTS WITH YOU (ME), MY DARLING,
FINALLY I'M SURE AND SO GLAD I'M CAUGHT
WHAT YOU SEE IN ME, WHAT YOU WANT ME TO BE,
WHAT WE HAVE COULD SURELY SET US FREE.

LIGHTS DOWN on BOOTS and JANE. LIGHTS UP on CELIA, MAX, RONNIE

RONNIE
Why would you want to give him another chance? What is WRONG with you people? *(To Celia)* Are you happy now?

CELIA
I don't think about that.

MAX
That's all I think about.

RONNIE
Well, you're halfway there. Now if we can just meet in the middle . . .

MAX
I'm there. I'm waiting . . . Are you happy, Celia? Please, think about it. For me—for us.

CELIA sings introspective, others freeze/lights dim

HAPPY

(CELIA)
AM I HAPPY? WHAT DOES HAPPINESS MEAN?
IS IT SUCCESS? GOOD WORKS? ROMANCE? SO,
AM I HAPPY? LIFE ISN'T ALL THAT IT SEEMS,
NOT EVERYONE WILL GET THE CHANCE. SO,

AM I HAPPY? HOW DOES ANYONE KNOW
WHEN TO RISK ALL THEY HAVE FOR ALL THE REST?
AM I HAPPY? OR AM I BEING SNOWED
JUST CAN'T TELL ANYMORE WHAT IS BEST.

GO AWAY, LET ME BE, GO AWAY, SET ME FREE,
I DON'T NEED YOU, CAN'T YOU SEE?
WHAT IS HAPPINESS? IT'S ONLY FOR SUCKERS.

AM I HAPPY? WHY SHOULD ANYONE CARE?
I NEVER HAND A CHOICE, CAN'T THEY SEE?
AM I HAPPY? JUST TO ASK IS UNFAIR.
HAPPY EVER AFTER WAS NEVER MEANT FOR ME.

GO AWAY, LET ME BE, GO AWAY, SET ME FREE
I DON'T NEED YOU, IT'S SO TRUE
WHAT IS HAPPINESS? IT'S ONLY FOR OTHERS.

I'M NOT HAPPY. I KNOW WHAT HAPPINESS MEANS.
IT'S NOT A RAINBOW CHASE FOR SUCCESS, THOUGH
I COULD BE HAPPY, WITH THE MAN OF MY DREAMS.
WHY IS THAT HARD FOR ME TO CONFESS? SO,

ARE YOU HAPPY? HOW DOES ANYONE KNOW
WHEN TO RISK ALL THEY HAVE FOR ONE LAST CHANCE? NO,
I'M NOT HAPPY, BUT I'M NOT BEING SNOWED.
IF I TAKE YOUR HAND, WE COULD TRY ONE MORE DANCE.

I AM HERE, LET ME STAY, FOR AN HOUR, FOR A DAY,
YES, I NEED YOU, NOW I SEE.
WHAT IS HAPPINESS? IT COULD BE FOR LOVERS.

CELIA
(*Still can't take the risk.*) It took me thirty years to build these walls. It'll take more than thirty minutes to pull them down.

> *LIGHTS UP ALL with crash from offstage, and TROY NOONAN enters from storage room. Troy is young, successful and effortlessly rich but unassuming, a totally nice guy who is clearly in love with RONNIE.*

MAX
Where'd you come from? How'd you get in here? *(Big reaction from everyone, surprised he's there)*

TROY
I opened the door.

FINGERS
Just like Gene Hackman in <u>The Heist.</u>

MABEL
That was a great movie.

TROY
Mother called, she was getting worried.

RONNIE
Gosh, your mother called? I couldn't meet her—is she really hissed off?

TROY
You worry too much about what she thinks. (*Hugs and kisses her*) I was worried, though.

BOOTS
But that door's jammed. I nearly broke my (*Looks at MABEL, and edits himself*) whatsis trying to get it open.

MAX
Nearly broke my whatsis, too.

JANE
Poor baby, does it hurt?

BOOTS
Only when I dance. (*Cuts a few steps.*)

MABEL
Then don't. No, I mean really—don't.

TROY
You have to push the door from the outside. It opens inward, never mind the crash bar on the inside. High school kids all know that. The back room used to be a make-out spot.

CELIA
(*Gathering things*) I'm out of here, people. It's been—strange. But I've got places to go, people to see—and a payroll to meet.

MAX
Sure. Time is money. So I hear.

MABEL
And I've always heard that money is . . .

EVERYONE
Comfortable!

MABEL
I was going to say, the root of all evil. But I'll take comfortable. Took me years to find comfortable. That's what makes me happy.

TROY

Speaking of found money, the feds just located a boatload of missing cash. It's been traced to some old-time mafia hit man, got caught about 20 or 30 years ago. Before my time. What I wouldn't give to have a crack at prosecuting a high profile case like that.

MUSIC begins under following lines.

RONNIE

Just wait, honey. You're the youngest assistant DA this county ever had. You're going places.

TROY

Just as long as you're beside me. *(He sings)*

THE PICTURE
THERE'S A PICTURE INSIDE MY HEAD
OF THE MAN I'M SPOZED TO BE.
AND AT NIGHT WHEN I'M IN MY BED
THAT PICTURE SPEAKS TO ME.
THERE'S A BABY THAT WILL MAKE US THREE
SHE'S PERFECT! SHE LOOKS JUST LIKE YOU.
THERE'S MY RONNIE—AND IT'S PLAIN TO SEE
YOU'RE THE PERFECT CHOICE, MY DREAMS CAME TRUE.

BECAUSE YOU FIT, YOU'RE PART OF THE PICTURE
WE BOTH FIT, WE'RE INSIDE THE FRAME.
THE WHOLE TOWN KNOWS WE'RE JUST THE RIGHT MIXTURE
CUZ WE'RE BOTH CAUGHT UP IN A CINDERELLA GAME.

MUSIC continues under following dialogue

RONNIE

Troy, I'm not pregnant. I'm sorry. I should have told you before but I –

TROY

Where are your wings? All angels have them.

BOOTS

That's great! I'm going to use that! *(He writes it down.)*

JANE

You're not going to need lines anymore. *(Takes note pad and tosses it, kisses him.)*

RONNIE
But Troy, I lied to you. I just didn't want to disappoint you—or your mother.

TROY
You didn't lie. You just anticipated the future a little. (*sings*)

BECAUSE YOU FIT, YOU'RE PART OF THE PICTURE
(TROY AND RONNIE) WE BOTH FIT, WE'RE INSIDE THE FRAME.
WHO CARES WHO THINKS WE'RE NOT THE RIGHT MIXTURE
I NEVER WANT TO LEAVE THIS CINDERELLA GAME.
I'M WORKING FOR THE DAY, MY ONE TRUE LOVE WILL SAY

(RONNIE)	(TROY)
(*spoken*) HE	(*spoken*) SHE

(BOTH *sung*) LOVE THE CHOICE THAT CHANGED THE LIVES WE HAD.

MAX
(*to TROY*) What was his name?

TROY
Who?

MAX
The mafia hit man, what was his name?

TROY
Joey . . . something, Vermicelli? Started with a V.

MAX
Venitucci.

TROY
That sounds right. But doesn't matter, anyway. The guy died in prison 15 years ago. That whole "family" went away pretty quick after they sent him up.

MAX and CELIA both react, he crosses to her.

FINGERS
Just like Humphrey Bogart in White Heat.

MABEL
That was Jimmy Cagney.

FINGERS
(*Big grin*) Adopt me. I need you.

MAX and CELIA look at each a long moment as music plays underneath—and finally kiss, love wins out. As song begins, each couple is wrapped up in each other.

CURVES (REPRISE)

(FINGERS sings to MAX)
THIRTY YEARS HAVE PASSED SINCE YOU LOST YOUR LOVE
BUT TODAY YOU GOT RID OF YOUR MASK.
SHOWED YOUR PAIN TO YOUR ONE TRUE LOVE
SO NOW I JUST GOTTA ASK.
WILL YOU RISK YOUR HEART, TAKE A CHANCE ON LOVE?
WILL YOU PLAN BEYOND TODAY?
CURVES COST YOU DEAR, BUT YOUR ONE TRUE LOVE
SAYS IT'S A PRICE SHE'LL GLADLY PAY.

(MABEL and FINGERS)
CURVES, WHEN THE ROAD SEEM STRAIGHTEST THERE'LL BE
CURVES, WHEN THE PATH SEEMS SAFEST THERE'LL BE
CURVES, WHEN YOUR PERFECT PLAN UNFURLS THE
CURVES WILL THROW YOU.
NERVES, WON'T HELP THE ROAD GET STRAIGHTER
SWERVES, DON'T HELP THE PATH TURN SAFER
EVERYONE SERVES A LIFE WITH CURVES.

(TROY sings to RONNIE)
I MADE MY PLANS, WITH MY ONE TRUE LOVE,
MAPPED EVERY STEP TO BE,
GRABBED LIFE WITH BOTH HANDS, FOR MY ONE TRUE LOVE,
NO ROLLING THE DICE FOR ME.

(MAX and CELIA)
BUT I STUMBLED AND FELL, THOUGH MY ONE TRUE LOVE
DIDN'T KNOW I'D LOST MY WAY,
AND I WENT TO HELL WHEN MY ONE TRUE LOVE
DIDN'T KNOW THE DEBTS I'D PAY.

(ALL singing in couples to each other)
CURVES, WHEN THE ROAD SEEM STRAIGHTEST THERE'LL BE
CURVES, WHEN THE PATH SEEMS SAFEST THERE'LL BE
CURVES, WHEN YOUR PERFECT PLAN UNFURLS THE
CURVES WILL THROW YOU.

NERVES, WON'T HELP THE ROAD GET STRAIGHTER
SWERVES, DON'T HELP THE PATH TURN SAFER
EVERYONE SERVES A LIFE WITH CURVES.

MABEL
(To Fingers) Come on, let's go home.

FINGERS
(Bad Bela Lugosi impression) "Home? I have no home…. Hunted."

MABEL
Bela Lugosi, 1955, <u>Bride of the Atom.</u>

FINGERS
(Beaming) Would you carry my lunchbox?

MABEL
(Taken aback, and then) I'd be honored. *(Taking it from him like a treasure)*

FINGERS
Yeah, let's go home.

CELIA
(Looking around at Maxine's Gym, then to Max) I'm already home.

JANE
I think I'll play hooky today. *(Hands Boots car keys)* You want to drive?

BOOTS
(Looks at keys) Chevy Bel Air?!

JANE
Celia, don't forget your sparkles. *(Refers to her shiny jacket on coat rack)*

CELIA
(To JANE) Why don't you keep it? I've outgrown it.

JANE
(Putting on the jacket). It fits!

BOOTS
Wow baby. *(Struggles for a line)* I'm speechless.

LIFE HAPPENS (NOTE, may use each verse as a curtain call, group bow at end of chorus)

(JANE & CELIA, Verse 1)
I GET (USED) TO BE THE GIRL WITH THE SPARKLES
I GET (GOT) TO SEE THE VIEW FROM THE TOP
TAKE MY PLACE, MAKE MY MARK, CUZ
DESTINY YOU CAN'T STOP.

(MABEL & RONNIE, Verse 2.)
I SAW MYSELF SWEET, AND SO RESERVED
WILL MAKE THIS WEALTH HELP THE DESERVED.
MUST TAKE MY PLACE, TIME TO SHARE!
I DON'T HAVE TIME TO SPARE
DESTINY YOU WON'T STOP.

(MAX & TROY—CHORUS)
LIFE HAPPENS, LIFE HAPPENS
LIFE HAPPENS THAT WAY
STAY TRUE TO INTENTIONS,
YOUR BEST INTERVENTIONS
GET PICKED FOR A WIN
JUST THAT WAY.

(BOOTS, FINGERS, Verse 3)
WE'VE GOT IT GOOD, IT'S PLAIN TO SEE
BET YOU WISH IT COULD BE YOU, NOT ME
WON'T TRADE MY PLACE, WOULDN'T DARE!
FINALLY SOMEBODY CARES
DESTINY NO ONE CAN STOP.

Verse twice, all singing parts, then . . .

CHORUS SUNG TWICE

(ALL)	(CELIA, DESCANT)
LIFE HAPPENS,	LIFE WITHOUT LOVE HAPPENS,
LIFE HAPPENS	LIFE GOES ON, IT HAPPENS
LIFE HAPPENS THAT WAY	LIFE SOMETIMES HAPPENS THAT WAY
STAY TRUE TO INTENTIONS,	FORGET YOU? WOULD NEVER HAPPEN,
YOUR BEST INTERVENTIONS	ALWAYS DREAMED OUR LOVE WOULD LIVE AGAIN
GET PICKED FOR A WIN	YOU SPARKLED MY HEART
JUST THAT WAY.	TODAY.

SUCK IT UP, SWEETHEART (*NOTE, may use as encore*)

(ALL)
SUCK IT UP, SWEETHEART
LUCKS A CROCK, SWEETHEART
WORK IT OUT SWEETHEART
NOTHING COMES FOR FREE
WHEN LIFE'S A BITCH SWEETHEART
AND YOU GOT THE ITCH SWEETHEART
TIME TO MAKE A SWITCH SWEETHEART
JUST REMEMBER ME.

END

MUSICAL NUMBERS

Act One

Overture (TACIT)

Auld Lang Syne (workout music) (TACIT)

1. Someone Must See Me (Jane)...81
2. The Picture (Ronnie)..83
3. Pitching Woo (Fingers, Boots)..85
4. You're the Chick for Me (Boots)...88
5. Curves (Maxine) 90
6. Dreams for Sale (Celia, Jane, Ronnie) 92
7. Life Happens (Company) 94

Act Two

Entracte (TACIT)

8. The Dream (Max, Celia) 99
9. Suck It Up, Sweetheart (All but Celia)..102
10. Pitching Woo, Reprise (Fingers, Mabel) 114
11. Silver Screen Blues (Fingers) 116
12. Poetry & Jazz (Jane, Boots)...118
13. Happy (Celia)...122
14. The Picture, Reprise (Troy, Ronnie)...124
15. Curves, Reprise (Company)...125
16. Life Happens, Reprise & Bows (Company)..127
17. Suck It Up, Sweetheart, Reprise/Encore/Exit (Company)....................133

1. Someone Must See Me

Frank Steele/Amy Shojai

3. Pitching Woo

4. You're The Chick For Me

Frank Steele/Amy Shojai

BOOTS

You're the chick for me! Hey there, be my ba-by. Please say yes or may-be may-be. I'm not like this with all the girls. Some-how with you it's diff'-rent. Mar-ry me, we'll raise an in-fant. A cu-tie like you with lots of curls. (spoken) Do ya play the pi-an-o? Bet cha do. Make yer own clothes? I know it's true. All the girls like you through and through. (sung) You're the chick for me! What's your sign? I'm a Lib-ra. Do you like pets? We'll buy a ze-bra. The sun is cap-tured in your hair. You own my heart, now own my li-fe. Just say "yes, I'll be your wife."-You're the blue rib-bon at the coun-ty fair.

Copyright © Frank Steele/Amy Shojai

7. Life Happens

9. Suck It Up Sweetheart

Amy Shojai/Frank Steele

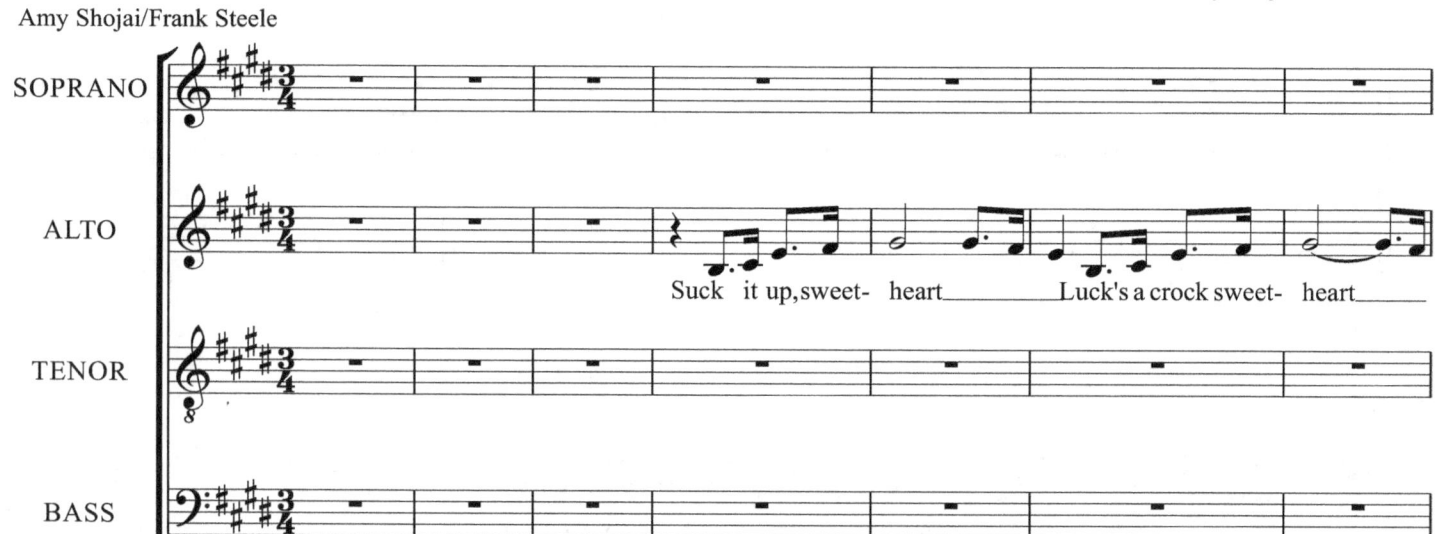

Copyright © Amy Shojai/Frank Steele

MABEL: "What were you thinking?..."

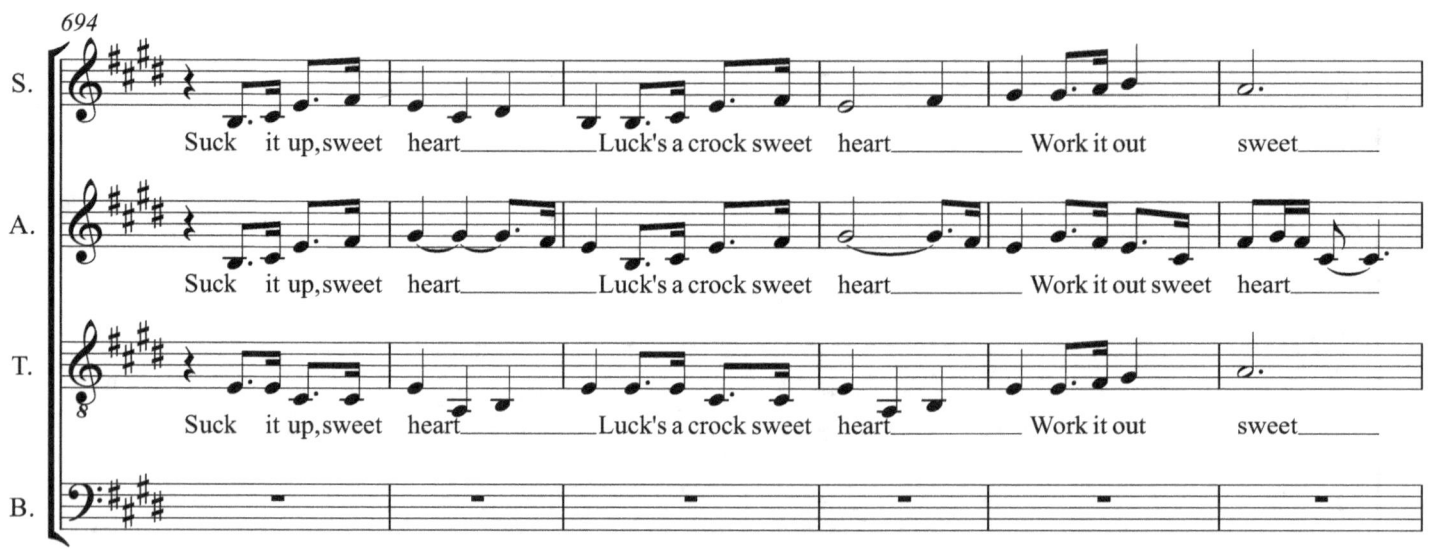

110

MABEL: "Just who doesn't notice you, Jane?..."

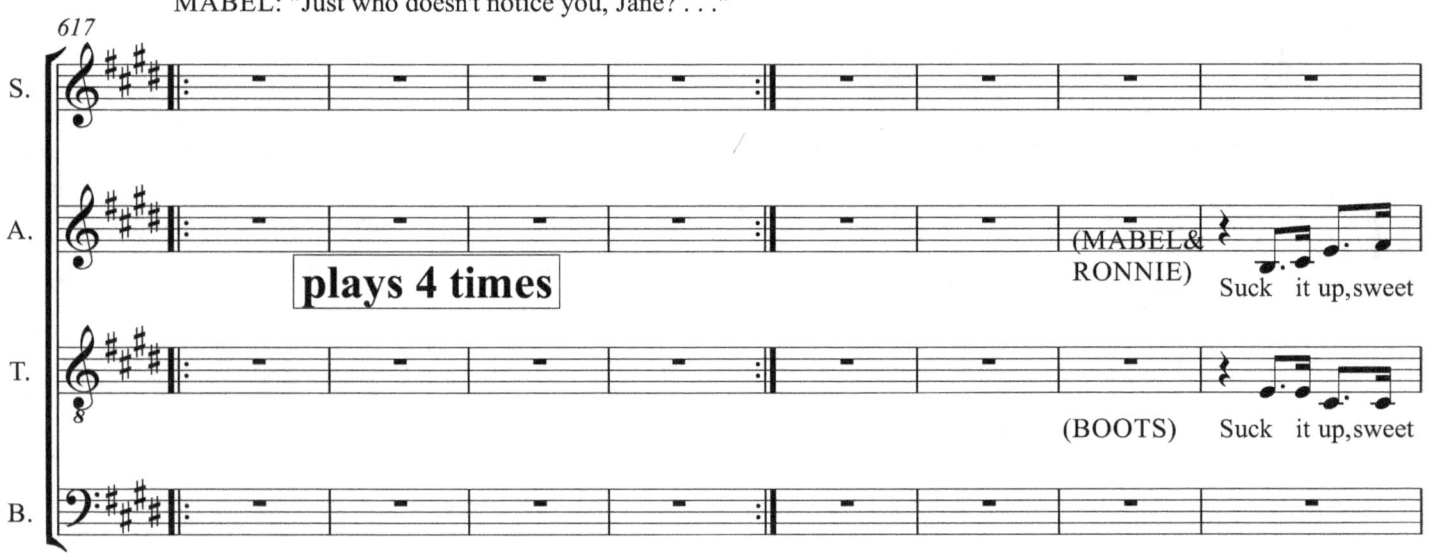

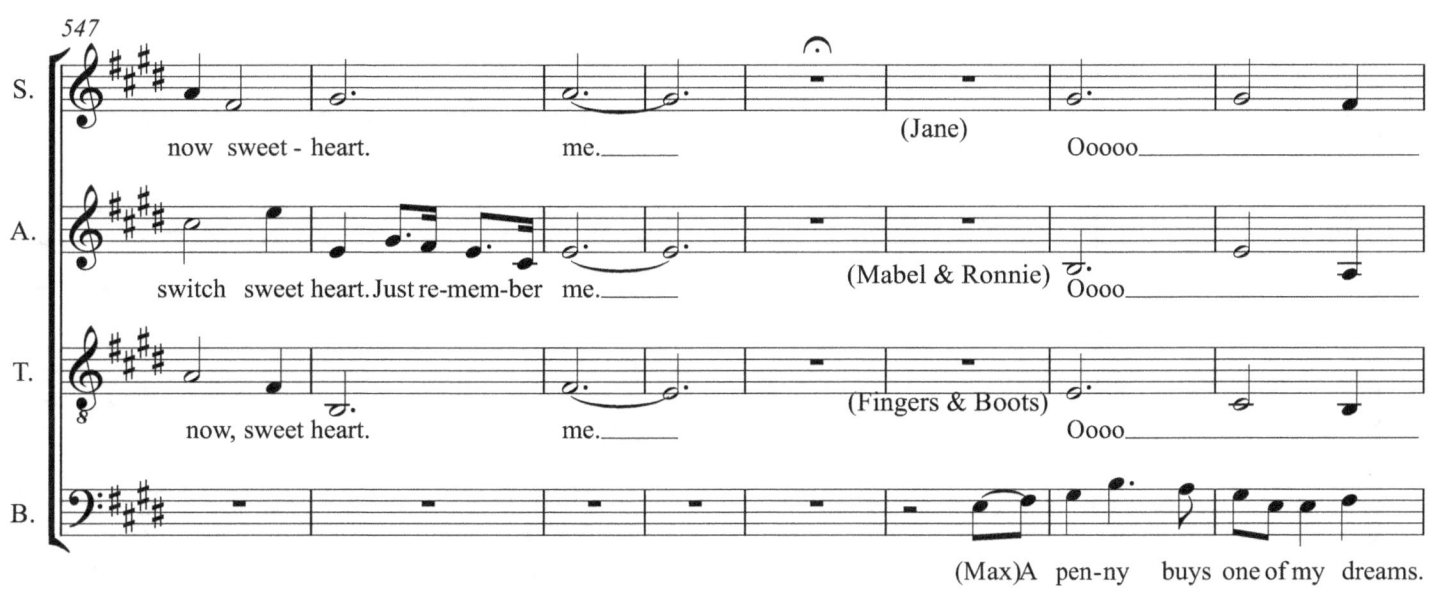

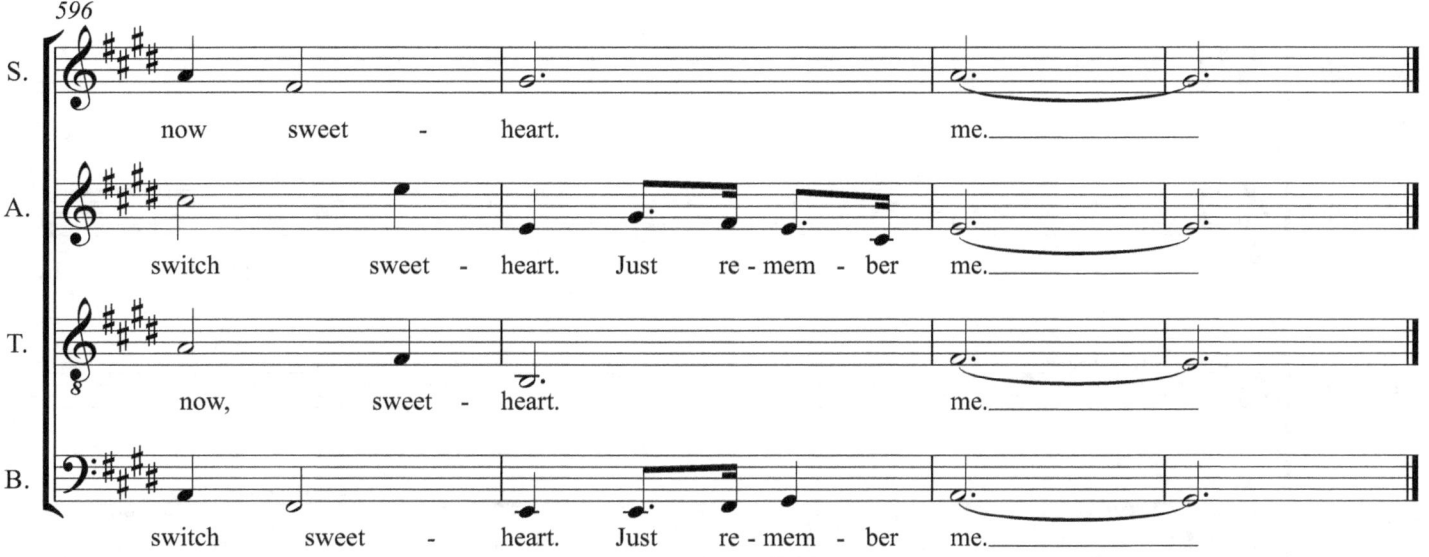

10. Pitching Woo--Reprise

11. Silver Screen Blues

Frank Steele/Amy Shojai

Copyright © Frank Steele/Amy Shojai

12. Poetry & Jazz

Amy Shojai/Frank Steele

JANE: I pre-fer to read my books, "pop-u-lar" was not in my sight. Po-et-ry made up for my lack of looks, in my pret-ty world, I'm a pret-ty girl, in my pret-ty world, where rhymes de - light.

BOOTS: I'm on my own all a-lone hustl-ing each nick-el and dime. No-thing to own dis-con-nect-ed phone, buy-ing each i-tem on time.

JANE: Ev'-ry day I teach a new verse, po-et-ry the lan - guage of love. But once a-lone I can't feel much worse. No one cares for me,

Copyright © Amy Shojai/Frank Steele

14. The Picture--Reprise

Amy Shojai/Frank Steele

TRO

There's a picture inside my head of the man I'm sposed to be. And at night - when I'm in my bed that picture speaks to me. There's a baby that will make us three. She's perfect! Looks just like you! There's my Ronnie and it's plain to see you're the perfect choice, my dreams came true. Because you fit, you're part of the picture. We both fit, we're inside the frame. The whole town knows - we're just the right mixture. - - And we're both caught up in a Cinda-rel-a game.

TROY & RONNIE

Because you fit, you're part of the picture, we both fit, we're inside the frame. Who cares who thinks___ we're not the right mixture - - I never want to leave this Cin-da-rel-la game. I'm working for the day my one true love will say,

(SPOKEN) "he" "she" loves the choice that changed the lives we had.

Copyright © Amy Shojai/Frank Steele

15. Curves--Reprise

Shojai/Steele · Shojai/Steele

FINGERS
Thirty years have past since you lost your love but today you got rid of your mask. -Showed your pain to your one true love so now-I've just got to ask. Will you risk your heart take a chance on love? Will you plan beyond today? Kurves cost you dear, but your one true love says It's a price she will gladly pay!

MABEL & FINGERS
Kurves - when the road seems straight-est there'll be Kurves - when the path seems saf-est there'll be Kurves when your perfect plan un-furls the Kurves will throw you. Nerves - won't help the road be straight-er swerves - don't help the path turn saf-er no one deserves to live with Kurves. - I made my plans with my one true love,

MAX & CELIA
mapped ev-ry step to be. Grabbed life with both hands for my one true love, no roll-ing the dice for me. But I stum-bled and fell though my one true love did-n't know that I'd lost my way. And I went to hell when my one true love did-n't know all the debts I'd pay.

AL
Kurves - when the road seems straight-est there'll be Kurves - when the path seems saf-est there'll be Kurves when your perfect plan un-furls the Kurves will throw you.

Copyright © Shojai/Steele

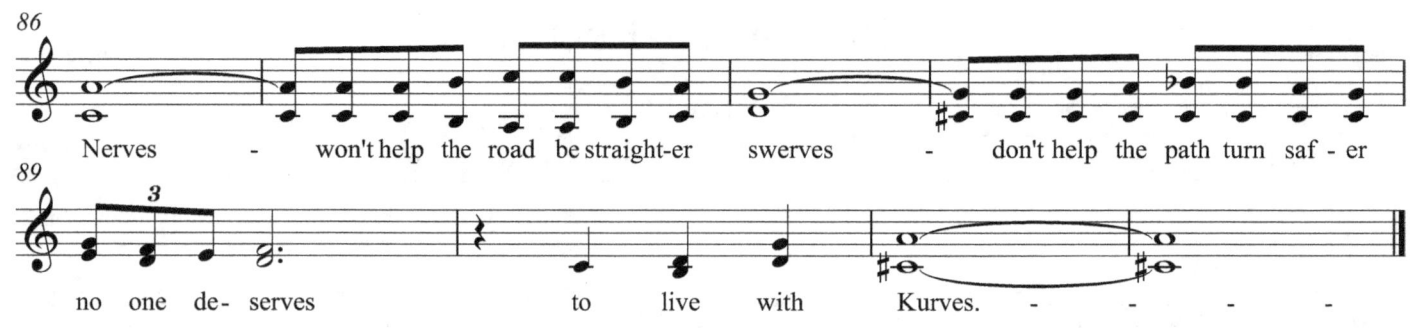

132

www.ingramcontent.com/pod-product-compliance
Lightning Source LLC
Chambersburg PA
CBHW081351080526
44588CB00016B/2449